The Vacation Home Exchange and Hospitality Guide

John Kimbrough

Kimco Communications
4242 West Dayton
Fresno, CA 93722

Published by:
>Kimco Communications
>4242 West Dayton
>Fresno, California 93722, USA

Copyright c 1991 by John Kimbrough
First Printing 1991
Printed in the United States of America

Publisher's Cataloging in Publication
(Prepared by Quality Books, Inc.)

Kimbrough, John, 1925-
>The Vacation Home Exchange and Hospitality Guide/
John Kimbrough.

p. cm
ISBN 0-9628199-0-5: $14.95

1. Home exchanging—Directories.
2. Vacation homes—Directories.

I. Title

TX907   647'.94
                                         LCCCN 91-90005

DISCLAIMER

This book is designed to provide accurate information in regard to the subject matter covered. It is sold with the understanding that the author and publisher are not engaged in rendering legal or other professional services. If legal advice or other expert assistance is required, the services of a competent professional should be sought.

While every effort has been made to assure the information in this guide is correct, it may contain errors both typographical and in content, and the information provided may change.

The author and Kimco Communications shall have neither responsibility nor liability with respect to any inconvenience, loss or damage caused, or alleged to be caused, by the information in the book.

TABLE OF CONTENTS

1
What About Vacation Home Exchanging?

With the spiralling costs of vacation lodging, the idea of vacation home exchanging is fast catching on. Only within the last two decades has this new approach to vacationing as a traveler, rather than as a tourist, mushroomed. An estimated 50,000 such travelers will become home exchange candidates this year through exchange clubs alone.

Thousands of available exchange homes are located in the United States, Canada, Mexico, the Caribbean, throughout Europe and many other countries abroad. Even the East European countries have now joined in. Exchanges offered range from the time-share condominium in Acapulco to the Victorian home in San Francisco, to a villa in southern France, or a Mediterranean dwelling

1

on the Costa del Sol. Perhaps something more exotic on a hidden island if that is to your liking.

Those who have exchanged homes say that the swap has all the advantages of traditional vacationing, and more, at a fraction of the cost. Practically the only expense is getting there.

(Usually a car is exchanged, too.)

Exchange clubs now publish directories of listings that make exchanging opportunities easily available to everyone for a nominal fee. Special clubs even cater to special interests and groups—exchanges for teachers, Rotary club exchanges, exchanges for the handicapped.

Listen to what an engineer, a translator/interpreter, and a retired salesman have to say about their experiences as home exchangers both domestically and abroad. Such comments are typical of those volunteered by exchangers when asked about their experiences at house-swapping.

"To the prospective first-time exchanger, I say, 'Go ahead. Take the risk. You are almost sure to like it.' I travel about 30 days a year on business. I don't need or want another hotel room when I'm on vacation." *(W.D., Orinda, CA, engineer; four exchanges)*

"Be ready for an exceptional experience. Imagine our surprise to be greeted by a domestic servant. This is unusual here in Canada—but not in Mexico." *(R.C., Ottawa, Canada, translator/interpreter; one exchange)*

"GO FOR IT. We have stayed in a 300-year-old fieldstone cottage in the Cotswolds, a remodelled Manor

House in Essex, an ultra-modern apartment in Bonn, and a comfortable chalet in Switzerland. What a variety! One should regard the exchange as an exciting opportunity to move out of the regular world. Great way to do it." *(D.B., Sacramento, CA, retired salesman; four exchanges)*

What Are the Reasons for Home Exchanging?

Most individuals use home exchanging for vacationing. The reasons for vacationing are, of course, as varied as the persons involved. Adventure, sight-seeing in exotic places, simple get-away, visiting the museums and tourist attractions are good enough reasons. Whatever the motive, the ventures usually go just as well, or better, using home exchanging, plus you enjoy a long list of added advantages. Experienced home exchangers point out the following special advantages of home exchanging over traditional travel or the package tour.

Economy

Economy is always the main advantage. Exchangers have learned that they can go farther on their vacations, stay longer, and set forth more frequently than the traditional traveler thanks to the cost savings.

With home exchanging, hotel room expenses, tipping, and related charges for such items as cleaning and laundry are eliminated. Even modest apartment rental in London or Paris will cost a minimum of $600-800 per week. And while the cost of rentals soars during desirable vacation months, the home exchange is oblivious to season. You get to vacation in choice spots during peak seasons, which otherwise would be cost-prohibitive. Expensive meals in high-priced restaurants are no longer part of your budget, except when you wish them to be. The reduced cost of lodging becomes especially noticeable if you take the children, or a group of any age.

A car is ordinarily exchanged which means no layout of $100 to 150 a week for the smallest car plus the added charges for mileage and insurance. With the exchanged car, gasoline is your only cost and mileage, as a rule, is unlimited, within reason, of course. While the cost of gasoline abroad generally runs higher than in the United States, the distances within and between the smaller host countries of Europe are much shorter than even between many states at home.

Home exchanging becomes especially relevant for the retiree, who is likely to be equity—rich with a comfortable paid-off home, the value of which has skyrocketed with inflation; but he or she may be travel-poor because of limited cash flow. The homeowner in this otherwise enviable situation could indulge in creative financing taking out an equity loan to finance travels, but this would be at the expense of elevated interest rates and renewed home loan payments. A better alternative is to use that attractive home as his ticket to travel, through creative home exchanging.

Comfort and Convenience

While economy is the major reason for home exchanging, many home exchangers are quick to say that there are other reasons just as important as, or more important than, the dollar savings. "Comfort" and "convenience"

are mentioned more often than anything else when veteran home exchangers talk about their experiences.
They like the comfortable home setting, usually away from tourist areas and city centers, where they can spread out in more than one room. You are able to unpack, do laundry and have coffee, drinks, snacks, meals on hand as you desire. You don't have to carry valuables with you or get them in and out of a hotel safe. The home quickly becomes your home and a convenient base where you can come and go at will and rest between small trips of 2 to 3 days about the area if so desired. A car is usually available on the spot.

The comfort and convenience of the "home away from home" over that of the hotel room become especially important if your stay is an extended one. An exchange home is ideal for the longer vacations. Most travelers do not care to stay in hotels for a month or two nor to eat out constantly.

Children

Not only does home exchanging make travel with children affordable, it also offers a number of other benefits for family travel. It gives the children a place to play, perhaps toys and games to play with and neighborhood children. It is a great advantage for a family not to have the children confined to a hotel room but to let them enjoy the extra space and maybe a yard. Often you can also use your exchange partner's babysitter with your children.

Freedom

Another home exchanging plus is the freedom to be a traveler and not a tourist. Exchangers like the individuality and the personalized approach to travel that home exchanging offers. Such travel is tailor-made for those who prefer to be independent travelers.

Home exchanging gives the traveler freedom to wander, dawdle, make last-minute changes because of weather or plain whimsy. You are not chained to the exchange home every night nor to a tour-group schedule. You can take loop-trips of several days or a week or more—and bed-and-breakfasts overnight—if you so desire. You are free to come and go at leisure without crowded buses or rapid tours.

The compulsion to see everything is eliminated, and you have time to enjoy your touring, even returning a second time to a favorite spot. You set your own itinerary and schedules lose their importance.

With exchanger permission, you can invite guests, friends or family to join you.

Live Like a Local

One of the main advantages of home exchanging is that you get to become a part of the country or neighborhood, absorb the culture, learn and make friends. The vacationer who travels as a tourist travels at a distance from locals, never quite getting beneath the surface. Because of this the tourist often misses out on things that he never suspects are there.

It is a different experience to feel you are living in a country and a part of it. You get to meet people in the real world—not the artificial world of the hotel/travel agent. Exchange partners often make arrangements for you to have invitations to friends' houses for dinner. It is common for neighbors to take you on tours and help acquaint you with customs, foods, the local stores and community.

For many people, these experiences mean more than any money they save on accommodations. Out of these experiences, you are apt to make long-term friends. Exchangers often report that they have been house guests of their exchangers in later years and that they always have a place to stay when in that area.

Who Goes On Vacation Home Exchanges?

Home exchanging as we know it today was developed in the early 1950's. Intervac International started it as a way for teachers in the Netherlands and Switzerland to swap homes during their summer holidays. It was not until the mid-70's that Intervac began advertising to non-teachers, since which time their listings have grown substantially.

In 1960 the Vacation Exchange Club was started by a high school teacher for American teachers. Two or three years later membership was thrown open to non-teacher subscribers, and their membership likewise began to multiply.

You need only take a look at the current directories of these two leading home exchange clubs to see how the current mix of home exchangers has shifted in recent years. While a large percentage of their listings are still teachers, probably 25 percent, the great majority of their listings cover the spectrum of professions and backgrounds. A quick scan of several pages from their directories shows such exchanger backgrounds as the following: dentist, architect, electrician, magistrate, police officer, floorer, psychologist, professor, social worker, doctor, engineer, manager, lawyer, merchant, bank employee.

The list goes on, and eventually manages to include almost everybody. Who goes on home exchanges? Anyone and everyone. People just like yourself.

The typical exchange party usually consists of two adults, but groups of four, seven or even more adults participating on one side of a vacation exchange are not uncommon. And a good third of the time, according to those exchangers you talk with, between one and several children, from infants to teenagers, accompany these adults.

Is it mainly retired people who have the time and means to participate in home exchanging? Not at all. Because they have flexibility of scheduling, retirees make up more than 25 percent of the home exchanging population. However, the great majority of exchangers are still actively employed and use exchanges for vacation travel.

What Is the Length of a Home Exchange?

The typical home exchange, depending upon its purpose and the flexibility of the exchangers lasts for two or three weeks. Few people exchange for one week or less, unless it is a domestic exchange that requires only a short flight or driving distance. However, such short stays can work well for the Vancouver resident who wants to spend a few days in San Francisco, for example, or for the ski buff who wants a winter week in Aspen. For trips abroad, usually two weeks is a minimum stay due to travel time and the expense of getting there. Yet, even abroad, the shorter stay of a week or ten days may fit in well with a necessary business trip of that duration. The month-long stay is popular, especially among retirees with more time to spend and teachers with a summer off. Two months or more are common among those with this amount of time available.

The most popular time of year with exchangers is summer, with fall preferred second. Since spring and winter seasons are least in demand, these two seasons offer more opportunity for those free to go then. Exchangers open to exchange any time of year enjoy the greatest opportunities of all.

How often do exchangers go on swaps. Experienced exchangers reveal that few of them limit themselves to just one exchange. The typical number of exchanges for one of the experienced group is at least four or five. You may just as easily find those who have been on seven or ten, or even 16 and 17 swaps and still planning more.

Where Do Exchangers Go?

The most popular areas of exchange for Americans are England (especially the London area) and France. Germany, Spain, Canada and domestic exchanges in the United States also rank high. It seems that half the home exchangers you talk to have done an exchange in England, and almost as many say they have made exchanges in the United States as well as abroad.

The most sought-after areas at home are California, Florida, New York, Massachusetts, Colorado and

Hawaii. However, club directories carry extensive listings in practically all of the 50 states, so the choice of domestic exchanges is wide.

Likewise, the choice of foreign countries for an exchange is wide-ranging. Other countries that show heavy listings in the club directories are the Netherlands, Belgium, Italy, Sweden, Denmark, Ireland, Switzerland and Austria.

Almost any country you can name offers numerous home exchange opportunities. Mexico, islands in the Caribbean, Greece and Israel are available. East European countries such as Yugoslavia, Czechoslovakia, Poland, Hungary and East Germany are now included. And if your taste runs to the little-known, far-away or exotic, check out the listings for exchanges in such places as Algeria, Liechtenstein, Polynesia, Iceland, Zimbabwe, Tasmania, India or Thailand.

What Kinds of Exchanges Are Made?

Most often, exchangers swap a primary residence for another primary residence. This residence may amount to a four-bedroom ranch-style house in Santa Barbara, a townhouse in Manhattan, an apartment in San Francisco, a flat in London, a cottage in the Cotswolds or a villa in Southern France.

Exchanges are not limited to primary residences, however. Frequently, a vacation property is used by one or both parties involved. A hunting lodge in Canada is swapped for a vacation home in Rosarita Beach, Mexico. Or the owners of that time-share property in Tahiti may decide they prefer Europe this summer. So they exchange their two weeks in Tahiti for a condominium or house on the Mediterranean.

Experienced home exchangers usually, sooner or later, work out their own creative approaches to home exchanging. By doing so they come up with a variety of exciting and economical itineraries and exchange combinations. These can amount to a round robin exchange among three or more parties in various locations. Or they can take the form of a serial exchange that follows one after the other. Some exchangers combine all the best of home exchange, bed-and-breakfast, rental or hospitality accommodations into one package to come up with the itinerary or extended stay that they want.

The possibilities for home exchanging are almost endless and are often suggested or offered by other home exchangers with whom you have formed friendships. Such creative exchanging calls for more planning and logistics, but exchange travelers find this an exciting part of the adventure.

What Surprises Can I Expect In Home Exchanging?

The idea of home exchanging leaves some prospective exchangers apprehensive and with reservations. How do I know what to expect? Am I in for any surprises, they ask? The answer to this question, according to experienced exchangers, is that you are in for a great many surprises—almost all pleasant ones.

A certain amount of risk is involved in any venture, but the exchange clubs say novices are concerned about the wrong things. The clubs tell us that in all their years of operation they have seldom had complaints about these prime concerns—theft, breakage, or abuse of your home.

Complaints from home exchangers are made up of lesser concerns, and these are rare. Different housekeeping standards, misrepresentation of accommodations, unexpected guests in the exchange party— these are some of the occasional downside.

With very few exceptions, home exchangers are reliable people just like yourself. They are usually professional people who are interested in the same considerations and have the same things at stake. After all, you are sharing each other's homes, cost-free, often with extra added favors such as car use or club privileges. This unique relationship creates a certain common bond of respect and responsibility.

This is not to say that every exchange experience goes without flaw. That ideal exchange you thought was certain may get canceled, perhaps for emergency reasons. Nor does it suggest you will find every detail of an exchange completely to your liking. This would be too much to expect. Unpleasantries, though not necessarily big ones, come with all travel territory, but they are best handled with a little flexibility on the part of the traveler. Go prepared to find something new, perhaps different or unexpected, but still exciting, at each turn of your itinerary. That is the way to get the most out of home exchanging.

Perhaps the best way for the novice to get a feel for what he may discover in his home exchanging adventure is to hear some of the pros and cons of exchanging volunteered by experienced exchangers. Exchangers asked to recount surprises, both pleasant and unpleasant ones, encountered in their home exchanging experiences typically list experiences such as those below. You can decide for yourself how the pros and cons balance out:

Pro: "Our home was left in immaculate condition. Our exchange partner made arrangements for us for golf times at several private clubs which otherwise would not have been accessible."
Con: "A few long distance calls were made by the exchange partner's nanny. Insignificant in the total picture."

Pro: "Our exchange home in Sienna, Italy was a million-dollar apartment in an 11th century building, one block from town square. Also the host arranged for us to attend the 'Pablo' horse race. He would not accept payment for four tickets. The tickets would have cost us $300."
Con: We thought our Italian exchangers were bringing a teen-age son and daughter. Son was teen-age, but also a 30-year old brother. Turned out very good."

Pro: "Once a full-time maid paid for by exchanger."
Con: "Once a very bad car."

Pro: "Exchangers left our house impeccable always— even with children. Our neighbors entertained the exchangers. One neighbor looked our German exchanger up on a recent trip and was entertained royally. Different cultures do things differently—That's the charm of exchanging."
Con: "One exchange. We found the care, feeding and cleaning up after two cats distasteful. Neighbors were supposed to do this, but they went on vacation."

Pro: "Beautiful, friendly neighbors."

Con: "Driving in England. It is very dangerous for an older American."

Pro: "Impossible to delineate. Being invited by the Sacrist of Ely Cathedral to climb to the roof of the 'lantern' (control tower). Another —walking into the communion at St. George's Chapel at Windsor and hearing the choir sing Vaughn William's 'Mass in G Minor'."

Con: "English washers and dryers are inadequate and time-consuming. You will end up at the laundromat, which fortunately they have plenty of. For a small extra fee, they will have your clothes sorted and bagged when you return."

Pro: "Two houses were very large and all near subway lines which connected all over the city. All exchange partners took care of our house and car."

Con: "One home was unsuitable for our two year old and a four year old. It had a sharp glass dining table and no window guards. My two year old found medicine which had not been put away. Another home had a very dirty kitchen floor—and no good place to read."

Pro: "Austria exchange ended delightfully with new friendships. One exchange in a small Italian village was an exceptional find. It was quaint, hard to find, and the people welcomed us. The restaurant, which was hidden away, was near 5-star."

Con: "One dwelling was old with accommodation not on a level with our home. Once there was damage, though minor, to the furniture."

Pro: "Visits to neighbors homes for the evening, tea or dinner. Escorted to local sights by neighbors." Con: "Walked into an exchange home saturated with smoke. We had not inquired."

Pro: "Chocolates and flowers left for us by exchangers—at both ends." Con: "None."

Pro: "Homes more luxurious than we expected." Con: "None."

Pro: "Nice clean house." Con: "Slight auto damage."

This feedback from home exchangers gives the exchange candidate an idea of what he may encounter in his house-swapping venture. It also alerts him to be aware of certain considerations in making an exchange and to plan accordingly.

What About Home Exchange Clubs?

By far, the majority of vacation home exchanges are made through exchange clubs. Clubs take the guesswork out of exchanging and provide valuable services to the would-be exchanger at nominal cost. For an annual fee of usually $50 or under, the home exchanger can get the club's directories which list not only his property but thousands of other exchange properties.

As an alternative to joining a club, you can run an ad in a newspaper, magazine or newsletter that reaches the desired area of exchange or a particular audience of potential exchangers. This might amount to an ad in the *Times of London*, a travel newsletter, or an outdoors/sports magazine (if you offer a fishing lodge in a choice location, for instance). Such advertising, except in specialized situations, greatly limits your chances of finding the exchange you want. This approach to home exchanging can work out great in certain instances. The fact is it usually does not. Most vacation home exchanges are arranged through listings in club directories.

Any number of exchange clubs exist for you to choose from. These clubs range from those with large general-interest memberships to the smaller clubs that offer more specialized services. Generally speaking, there are two types of home exchange clubs or services. These are the directory clubs and the full-service clubs.

The directory clubs comprise the larger of the two groups. As the name indicates, directory clubs publish directories of listings for subscribers. The subscribers are responsible for making contacts and arranging their own exchanges. Subscribers to the directory clubs receive one or more directories yearly that list homes available for exchange. The subscriber may choose to receive the directories without listing his own property if he so wishes. This will give him access to exchanges offered, but, of course, his property will have no exposure with potential exchangers. An unlisted subscriber must take all the initiative for contacting prospective exchangers.

For user convenience, listings in the directories are categorized by country and sometimes by city or area. Listings will usually include all the relevant information about an exchanger—name, address, telephone, profession, area of exchange preferred, time preferred, and details about features of the home offered.

From this point on, it is up to the subscriber to take the initiative for contacts, responses and exchange arrangements. However, the directory clubs do frequently step in to assist members when last-minute emergencies or special situations arise. Full-service clubs, on the other hand, take on the task of locating and arranging exchanges for their subscribers, who do not receive a directory. Accordingly, the fees for these services run considerably higher than those of the directory clubs. Full-service clubs comprise a small group, with a high attrition rate, and only a limited number of such clubs are currently in operation.

Which Exchange Club Should I Join?

Before the would-be exchanger puts down his money on an exchange club, he should know something about the particular club and have an awareness of the other clubs available and what they have to offer. Then he can make an informed choice among all the possibilities and open up the most options for his desired exchange.

How long has the club been in business? What kind of track record does it have? How many listings does it have? In what areas are the listings located? Are the listings mainly at home or abroad? What kind of subscriber mix does the club have? What countries are included? How many opportunities exist in the country or countries of your choice? Is the club largely an exchange service, a rental service, or both? These are important considerations that will affect your exchange opportunities.

What is the right club for you? That depends upon what you are looking for. Two of the directory clubs—the Vacation Exchange Club and Intervac International—offer you the most listings, therefore the most choices. Both clubs have a balance of listings, USA versus foreign, that is generally favorable. However, Vacation Exchange Club has 30 to 40 percent of its listings in the USA which is favorable for both American and European exchangers. Intervac International directories carry four times as many listings for countries abroad as for the USA, which is more favorable for Americans wishing an exchange abroad than for foreign exchangers.

If you wish an exchange in the Scandinavian countries (aside from Denmark), Intervac is the only club with a substantial number of listings for that area. If you prefer Australia or New Zealand, then the Vacation Exchange Club (as well as the Worldwide Home Exchange club) has the most to offer. You will settle for nothing less than an exchange in Brazil? Then you are back to Intervac International.

Should your interest lie more in the long-term exchange, especially in the London area, then Loan-A-Home club, with its emphasis on long-term exchanges and rental options, may offer you the most.

You want to arrange a home exchange but would like to remain within your own professional circle of exchangers? Teacher Swap is exclusively for teacher exchanges, mainly summer and vacation exchanges in the USA. Likewise, Loan-A-Home listings draw heavily upon educators and businessmen, but concentrate on exchanges abroad.

If you want to avoid the work, or fun, of arranging your own exchange, you can turn to the full-service clubs. You will have less selection with the full-service clubs, and they usually specialize in a few areas such as Italy, France or England. But if their specialty and selection fit in with your interests and you don't mind the extra fee, that may be the way for you to go. The trick is to check out each club's profile—its listings in individual countries, its emphasis, its strengths and weaknesses— to see how these items dovetail with your interests.

The home exchanging scene is a fast-changing one that in recent years has seen numerous new clubs spring up, established clubs change hands or consolidate with others, and a good many clubs shift their emphasis or disappear altogether.

The chapters following give updated profiles of vacation home exchange clubs in the USA and abroad. (A later section of the guide gives similar profiles for hospitality exchange clubs and homestay programs.) A familiarity with these clubs and their profiles will better enable both the novice and the experienced home exchanger to find that desired ideal home exchange whether it be their first, or fifth, or upcoming fifteenth such adventure.

2
Vacation Exchange Club and Directory Group Association

While the Directory Group Association numbers more than 20 affiliates world-wide, the Vacation Exchange Club (located in Youngstown, Arizona until recently), now headquartered in Hawaii, is the main affiliate, accounting for at least a third of the DGA listings.

The Vacation Exchange Club was first instrumental in forming the Directory Group Association. This club introduced home exchanging to the U.S. market and has been responsible for supplying the U.S. directory listings. This has helped create a favorable mix of subscribers who were previously mainly European. For these reasons, the Vacation Exchange Club receives focus as the prime DGA representative.

Vacation Exchange Club

P.O. Box 820
Haleiwa, HI 96712
Phone: Toll Free: 1-800-638-3841
In Hawaii: 638-8747
Fax: 1-808-638-5184
CompuServe: 72520,1414
Genie MBEAR

Directors:

Karl and Debby Costabel

Started:

1960—Vacation Exchange Club is the oldest home exchange agency in the United States.

Size:

Vacation Exchange Club is the largest single home exchange agency in the world. Vacation Exchange is an affiliate of the Directory Group Association which publishes yearly directories offering some 6,000 listings in 50 countries. About 2,000 of these listings are Vacation Exchange Club subscribers in the United States. (The Hawaii Home Interchange which previously operated as an independent sub-unit under Vacation Exchange has been absorbed into VEC. Likewise, the VCA Exchange club that as an affiliate of DGA handled Yugoslavia is now included in the Vacation Exchange Club.)

Subscription Fees: (annually)

Listed subscribers:	$50
Unlisted subscribers:	$55
Optional photo:	$12

The all-inclusive fees cover first class post paid shipping of the directories.

Directories:

Vacation Exchange Club publishes two directories each year—in February and April. (February is the main directory with April being the supplemental one.) Your home is listed in either the February or the April directory depending upon when it is received. Updated listings are available to members free of charge via CompuServe, GEnie, MCI Mail and Internet, year round. Vacation Exchange Club plans to publish an additional directory of exclusively USA listings for domestic exchangers.

Types of Listings:

Directory listings include home exchange, hospitality exchange, hospitality offered, youth hospitality and exchange, bed-and-breakfast, rental, travel companion, house-sitting, au pair (room and board for child-care services). The majority of listings are for primary home exchanges, but vacation and time-share properties are also offered for exchange.

Directory listings that have facilities for the handicapped are coded "hp." However, the possibility always exists that a listing not coded "hp" has facilities adequate for the handicapped exchanger. It does no harm to inquire.

Exchanger Profile:

The exchangers are largely upscale, professional, about 25 percent being teachers/educators.

Subscriber Mix:

Foreign listings:	60%
USA listings:	40%

This creates a favorable mix for both American and foreign exchangers.

Foreign Listings Profile:

England, popular with home exchangers, shows the most foreign listings, more than 500 in current directories. The London area, especially, is popular with exchangers, with a third of the listings for England in greater London.

West Germany, likewise, is a favorite with exchangers, presenting almost as many listings as England. Belgium offers more than 400 listings, with both the Netherlands and France indicating about 300 each. Canada is next with some 250 and Spain and Italy follow with 100 plus listings each.

Yugoslavia has been active in the home exchange program for several years and in current directories lists almost 80 exchanges. Yugoslavia is considered a "financial" hot-spot for economic travel in the 90s.

Denmark, Australia, Ireland and Mexico each give sizeable directory listings ranging between 40 and 95. The East European countries of East Germany, Czechoslovakia, Hungary and Poland are now also showing up.

More exotic places represent a sprinkling of listings: the Channel Islands, Guadeloupe, Turkey, the Virgin Islands, Morocco, Thailand, Senegal, Polynesia, Zimbabwe.

U.S.A. Listings Profile:

California is the most popular state with home exchangers. It shows over 600 listings in the recent directories. Florida is the next most popular, offering almost 300.

New York State has more than a 100 listings, most of these in greater New York City. Massachusetts shows more than 100.

Hawaii, with about 80 offerings and Colorado, with some 75, are popular exchange states in the West.

Midwestern and central states show the fewest domestic listings. However, 42 of the 50 states are represented with at least one or more listings in the current directories.

Club Strengths and Weaknesses:

Vacation Exchange Club is well-established, with a large base of upscale subscribers both at home and affiliated abroad. From the start, the Directory Group Association directed its European advertising toward professional people with significant incomes. A favorable balance of domestic and foreign subscribers offers advantages to those on both sides of the Atlantic. Many of their European subscribers wish to make exchanges in the USA and are able to afford them.

Vacation Exchange Club offers more listings than its rivals in the United States, Germany, Canada and Belgium. It also has substantial listings in the United Kingdom, France, Netherlands, Spain and Italy. New Zealand

24

and Australia are represented with significant listings in its directories, and South Africa shows strength only among its listings.

While strong in Denmark, the Vacation Exchange Club has limited representation in the other Scandinavian countries of Sweden and Norway, with only token listings for Finland. Likewise, the club offers few exchange opportunities in the Caribbean, and South America is untapped.

Directory Group Association Affiliates

The Directory Group Association, to which Vacation Exchange Club belongs, and of which it is the largest member, has branches in 20 countries outside the United States. The group prefers that subscribers join the club within their own country. Regardless of which DGA club you join, you get the same directory as all other subscribers.

The following is a list of the DGA exchange club affiliates in the various countries. The number of listings indicates those offered by each country in directories for the most recent year.

AUSTRALIA   International Home Exchange
DAT/TRAVEL
Level 2, 17 Sydney Road
Manly NSW 2095
Australia
Phone: (61) 8-232-2022

Listings - 68

BELGIUM	Taxistop
	Onderbergen 51
	B-9000 Gent
	Belgium
	Phone: (32) 91-232310

Listings - 425

BRAZIL	Brazil Home Exchange
	Rua Teofilo Otoni 44
	Rio de Janeiro
	Brazil
	Phone: (55) 21-2330518

Listings - None

CANADA	West World Holiday Exchange
	1707 Platt Crescent
	North Vancouver, BC VJ7 1X9
	Canada
	Phone: (1) 604-987-3262

Listings - 268

Subscription Fees:

Listed subscriber:	$54.50 CDN
Unlisted subscriber:	$45.50 CDN
Optional photo:	$10.00 CDN

Insurance is included in the above fees. The insurance consists of coverage for the following: personal liability, property damage, legal aid and emergency accommodation if the exchange home is temporarily uninhabitable.

CYPRUS	Homelink International
	P.O. Box 3110
	Limassol
	Cyprus
	Phone: (357) 51-54371

Listings - 10

DENMARK   Dansk Boligbytte
                 Hesselvang 20
                 DK-2900 Hellerup
                 Denmark
                 Phone: (45) 1-610405

                 Listings - 95

FRANCE   Sejours
                 Bel Ormeau 409, Ave. Jean Paul-Coste
                 13100 Aix-en-Provence
                 France
                 Phone: (33) 42384238

                 Listings - 312

GERMANY   Holiday Service
                 Ringstrasse 26
                 D-8608 Memmelsdorf 1
                 Germany
                 Phone: (49) 951-43055

                 Listings - 487

GREAT BRITAIN   Homelink International
                 2 Westmoreland Avenue, Wyton
                 Huntingdon, CAMBS PE17 2HS
                 England
                 Phone: (44) 480-457936

                 Listings - 560
                 Listings - 497 England (150 in London proper)
                 Listings - 44 Scotland
                 Listings - 19 Wales

IRELAND   Holiday Exchange International
                 95 Bracken Drive
                 Portmarnock, Co. Dublin
                 Ireland
                 Phone: (353) 1-462598

                 Listings - 65

27

ISRAEL   Israel Home Exchange
                    44 Louis Marshall Str.
                    Tel Aviv 62000
                    Israel
                    Phone: (972) 3-445407

                    Listings - 28

ITALY   Casa Vacanza
                    Via San Francisco 170
                    I-35121 Padova
                    Italy
                    Phone: (39) 49-38664

                    Listings - 131

NEATHERLANDS Land. Org. Vakantie-Woningruil
                    Kraneweg 86A
                    NL-9718 JW, Groningen
                    Netherlands
                    Phone: (31) 50-132424

                    Listings - 228

NEW ZEALAND   International Home Exchange
                    P.O. Box 38615
                    1 Peach Parade, Ellerslie
                    New Zealand
                    Phone: (64) 9-522-2933

                    Listings - 18

NORWAY   Norsk Boligbytte
                    95 Kjelsas
                    N-0401 Oslo 4
                    Norway
                    Phone: (47) 2-158019
                    Listings - 25

PORTUGAL Homelink International
100 Rua Vasconceles & Castro 2-d
4760 V.N. Famalicao
Portugal
Phone: (351) 52.57160

Listings - 1

SOUTH AFRICA International Home Exchange
P.O. Box 188, Claremont
Cape Town 7735
South Africa
Phone: (27) 21-614334
Listings - 36

SPAIN Viajes Calatrava
Cea Bermudez 70
E-28.003, Madrid
Spain
Phone: (34) 1-4494797

Listings - 135

SWEDEN Svensk Bostadsbyte
Hesselvang 20
DK-2900 Hellerup
Denmark
Phone: (45) 31610405

Listings - 28

SWITZERLAND Holiday Exchange Club Schweiz
Asylstrasse 24
CH-8810 Horgen
Switzerland
Phone: (41) 1-7251047

Listings - 29

3
Intervac International Exchange Club

Intervac International is the other giant among directory home exchange clubs, with over 8,000 listings in 34 countries. The total listings of Intervac International are larger than those of the Directory Group Association.

However, the listings of Intervac International are more evenly divided among several of its leading branches world-wide. No single affiliate holds prominence as does Vacation Exchange Club (USA) in the Directory Group Association, with its one-third of the total DGA listings.

Intervac International

Box 12066
S 29112 Kristianstad
Sweden
Telex: call Telebox S 16577 and begin with
Telebox = Intervac. S/Intervac

Started:

1953 —Intervac is the oldest of the home exchange clubs.

Size:

Intervac is the largest home exchange network in the world. Its directories carry some 8,000 listings yearly. However, none of its individual affiliates carry listings that compare in size with those of the Vacation Exchange Club (USA) of the Directory Group Association.

Subscription Fees: (annually)

Listed subscribers:	$45.00
SENIORS (62+)	$40.00
Unlisted subscribers:	$55.00
SENIORS (62+)	$50.00
Optional photograph:	$10.00

Directories:

Intervac publishes three directories annually—in February, April and June. Your home is listed in one of the directories (unless you opt for all 3 directories), and you will receive all three directories in either case. The February directory carries the bulk of their exchange listings, with the other two directories being supplemental.

The June directory gives last-minute summer exchange opportunities. This directory also carries reference numbers of people in the prior two directories who are still looking for an exchange. Starting June 8 each year, a "late service" is provided, which you may contact by telephone or mail. This service keeps an up-to-date list of people still needing an exchange. The main directory lists separately those subscribers seeking a long-term exchange, of more than three months.

Types of Listings Included:

Intervac listings include home exchange, hospitality exchange, hospitality offered, youth hospitality and exchange, house guests, rental, house sitting, bed and breakfast, week-end or other short-term exchange and open to offers. The majority of listings are for primary home exchanges.

Exchanger Profile:

Upscale, professional, a large percentage of teachers/educators (an estimated 1/3 or more).

Subscriber Mix:

| Foreign listings: | 80% |
| USA listings: | 20% |

This creates a favorable exchange ratio for the American exchanger who wishes to go abroad but is less favorable for the foreign exchanger to come to the USA.

Foreign Listings Profile:

Intervac now has more listings in England than does the Directory Group Association. Its recent main directory lists more than 600 entries for England, with the two supplemental directories carrying another 500, for a total of 1,100-plus listings in England.

France shows even more listings than England, with 800 in the main directory and another 600 in the supplemental ones.

Sweden is also strong with more than 700 entries in the current directories. (This is to be expected since Sweden is the international headquarters for Intervac.)

A number of other countries show substantial listing strength. Denmark, the Netherlands, Spain, Switzerland, and West Germany indicate over 300 each. Austria, Ireland and Italy about 200-300 opportunities per country. Belgium, Canada, Finland and Norway show 100-200 listings each. And Australia, Brazil, Greece and Portugal offer 30-100 exchanges.

Intervac also has its lesser group of exotic listings from such areas as Iceland, India, the Caribbean, Luxembourg, Hong Kong, Portugal, Zimbabwe and the Republic of the Congo.

Intervac directories carry a special section of listings for homes in the United Kingdom which may be suitable for disabled guests. Their directories for the current year contain such listings in England (27), Scotland (5), New Zealand (1). Those listings in areas outside the United Kingdom which have facilities for the handicapped are coded "hp." Absence of the "hp" coding does not mean that the exchange home might not have adequate facilities for the handicapped guest. An inquiry could be worthwhile.

USA Listings Profile:

California is the strongest area, with almost 600 listings in the directories for the current year. Florida is next with about 200 listings, and the states of New York, Massachusetts and the District of Columbia indicate about 100 listings each. Texas, Hawaii and Colorado show some 50 listings per state.

Club Strengths and Weaknesses:

Intervac International is the oldest of the home exchange clubs, with a large established base of subscribers in European countries. Intervac has more listings than the Directory Group Association in the following areas: Austria, Denmark, Finland, France, Ireland, Italy, the Netherlands, Norway, Portugal, Spain, Switzerland and the United Kingdom. Intervac is also established in South America, with 70 or so current listings for Brazil. The DGA is not yet established in that area.

Intervac's main drawback is that the club does not have a favorable balance of subscribers in the United States to offer their European subscribers. The membership is made up of 80 percent European and 20 percent USA subscribers. This ratio is especially favorable for USA subscribers because it gives them access to more foreign listings.

Intervac International Affiliates

Intervac International consists of independently owned affiliates located in 26 countries. The same directory of listings goes to all subscribers no matter which club you join. Intervac prefers that you join the club within your own country.

The following is a list of the Intervac affiliates worldwide. The total number of listings offered by each country in the directories of the current year are indicated.

AUSTRALIA

Intervac Australia
P.O. Box 684
Manly NSW 2095
Australia
Phone: (02) 9603566

Listings - 34

AUSTRIA

Intervac Austria
Amselweg 4
A 9100 Wolkermarkt
Austria
Phone: (042) 32/2147

Listings - 195

BELGIUM

Intervac Belgium
(French-speaking provinces)
Keukenlaan 7
B 1600 Sint-Pieters-Leeuw
Belgium
Phone: (02) 3773256

(Dutch-speaking provinces)
Lindenberglaan 26
B 1960 Sterrebeek
Belgium
Phone: (02) 7315202
Listings - 113

BRAZIL	Intervac Brazil
	Avenue Rio Branco 245, Room 1805
	CEP 20040 Rio de Janeiro (RJ)
	Brazil
	Phone: (021) 240-3725

Listings - 74

CANADA	Intervac Canada
	606 Alexander Crescent NW
	Calgary, Alberta T2M4T3
	Canada
	Phone: (403) 284-3747

Listings - 159

DENMARK	Intervac Denmark
	Boite Postale 3
	L-8201 Mamer G.D.
	Luxembourg
	Phone: (0352) 310724

Listings - 307

FINLAND	Intervac Finland
	Kellosilta 7
	SF 00520 Helsinki 52
	Finland
	Phone: (0) 1502484

Listings - 101

FRANCE	Intervac France, Algerie, Tunisie
	55 rue Nationale
	F 37000 Tours
	France
	Phone: (047) 202057
	Telex: 751657 EUROVAC

Listings - 1374

GERMANY	Intervac Germany Verdiweg 2 7022 Leinfelden-Echterdingen Germany Phone: (0711) 75F46069 Listing - 336
GREAT BRITAIN	Intervac Great Britain 6 Siddals Lane Allestree, Derby DE3 2DY England Phone: (0332) 558931 Listings - 1102
GREECE	Intervac Greece Fintiou 20 Athens 11253 Greece Phone: (01) 8678917 Listings - 51
ICELAND	Intervac Iceland Nybylavegur 42 200 Kopavogur Iceland Phone: (354) (1) 44684 Listings -11
IRELAND	Intervac Ireland Phillipstown, Ballymakenny Road Drogheda Ireland Phone: (041) 37969 Listings - 234

ISRAEL	Intervac Israel P.O.B. 2045 Herzliya 46120 Israel Phone: (972) 52559170 Listings - 3
ITALY	Intervac Italy Via Oreglia 18 40047 Riola (BO) Italy Phone: (051) 910818 Listings - 283
JAPAN	Intervac Japan 1-9-10 Nishiwaseda, Shinjuku Tokyo 160 Japan Phone: (03) 2057146 Listings - 12
LUXEMBOURG	Intervac Luxembourg Boite Postale 3 Luxembourg Phone: (352) 310724 Listings - 12
NETHERLANDS	Intervac Netherlands Paasberg 25 6862 CB Oosterbeek Netherlands Phone: (085) 341187 Listings - 446

NORWAY

Intervac Norway
Fagerlivigen 9
N 2800 Gjovik
Norway
Phone: (061) 79185

Listings - 118

POLAND

Intervac Poland
Al. Kalningradzka, 43 m 55
10437 Olsztun
Poland
Phone: (89) 332464

Listings - 14

PORTUGAL

Intervac Portugal
Rua Ignacio de Sousa 23
R/C Do.
1500 Lisboa
Portugal
Phone: (01) 785179

Listings - 44

SPAIN

Intervac Spain
Consell de Cent, 226, 1o, 3a
Barcelona
Spain
Phone: (03) 253.31.71

Listings - 378

SWEDEN

Intervac Sweden
Box 33
S.55112 Jonkoping
Sweden
Phone: (036) 128205

Listings - 796

SWITZERLAND	Intervac Switzerland-Liechtenstein Zilstr. 74 a CH-9016 St. Gallen Switzerland Phone: (07) 354910

Listings - 301

USA	International Home Exchange INTERVAC U.S. P.O. Box 190070 San Francisco, CA 94119 USA Phone: (415) 435-3497 FAX: (415) 386-6853

Listings - 1553

(Note: The Intervac affiliate, Interservice Home Exchange Inc., Glen Echo, MD, has been absorbed by the San Francisco affiliate.)

4
Other Directory-Driven Exchange Clubs

Aside from the Directory Group Association and Intervac International exchange networks, a good many other directory exchange clubs are available to the home exchanger.

Many of these smaller, usually non-affiliated clubs, have their own specialties or areas of concentration and may offer home exchange opportunities that fit your needs or interests better than the larger DGA or Intervac group. The Rotary Home Exchange, Loan-A-Home, and Worldwide Home Exchange Club are some of the other directory clubs that you will want to check out for their particular variety of listings and services.

International Fellowship of Rotarians Home Exchange

P.O. Box 1794
Santa Ana, CA 92702

Director:

Joseph E. Irvine

Started:

1976—Founded by the Rotary Club of Santa Ana North, California.

Size:

The Rotary Home Exchange directory for the current year lists 259 members.

Subscription Fees: (annually)

Listed subscriber:	$15.00
Photo:	$ 5.00

Directories:

The Rotary Home Exchange publishes one directory yearly that is received by subscribers in February. Listings in the directory are limited to Rotarians. This does not necessarily mean that listed subscribers will not exchange with non-Rotarians who have access to the directory listings. Non-Rotarians may obtain a copy of the directory by sending in a $15 subscriber fee.

The directory, unlike those of many exchange clubs, is easily readable with detailed, non-coded listings. The name of the subscriber's Rotary club and his classification (profession) are given, along with a description of his home and the areas or countries of exchange requested.

Types of Listings Included:

Listings include home exchange of primary residence, resort property and mobile homes.

Exchanger Profile:

Upscale, professional. All listed subscribers are Rotarians.

Subscriber Mix:

Foreign listings:	35%
USA listings:	65%

Foreign Listings Profile:

Rotary Home Exchange has listings in more than a dozen foreign countries. Most of these listings are found in England (35 listings for the current year) and Canada (31 listings). Australia and New Zealand show combined listings of 16. Token numbers of exchanges are available in the remaining countries: Denmark, France, India, Israel, Japan, Scotland, Turkey and West Germany.

43

USA Listings Profile:

USA listings are located in 36 of the states, with California providing the most (38 current listings) and with Florida the runner-up (25 listings).

Club Strengths and Weaknesses:

Rotary Home Exchange provides an opportunity for Rotarians and their families to become involved in the life-style of other Rotarians and their families, both at home and abroad. This serves a special purpose for those exchangers who identify more readily with members of their own group or profession.

The balance of domestic and foreign listings is favorable for those Rotarians from the USA who wish to exchange within their own country but less favorable for those who wish to go abroad. The balance offers special opportunities for those Rotarians abroad who wish to exchange in the USA.

The club's main limitation is that the listings are restricted to Rotarians.

Loan-A-Home

2 Park Lane - 6E
Mount Vernon, NY 10552
Phone: (914) 664-7640

Director:

Muriel Gould

Started:

1968

Size:

Loan-A-Home exchange club directories carry 500-600 listings per year.

Subscription Fees: (annually)

Current directory and a supplement: $35.00
(June directory & Sept. supplement)
            OR
(Dec. directory & March supplement)
All four issues: $45.00

Directories:

Loan-A-Home publishes two directories and two supplements per year. The June and December directories carry the bulk of the listings. September and March issues are supplements.

Types of Listings Included:

The listings include home exchange and rentals, with emphasis on rentals and long-term occupancy. The specific, long-term needs of many of the club's clients are difficult to meet through exchanges. Because of this, rental figures are listed wherever available. However, an exchange is always possible, even where a rental figure is quoted. The listing describes your HOUSING WANTED needs: location, time period and number of bedrooms.

Exchanger Profile:

Subscribers are mainly members of the international academic and business communities, and their families, who need temporary housing. They include university professors, medical and research personnel, and scholars in many fields who are planning to take a sabbatical abroad or in another domestic city. More and more often now, the director says, the clientele also include retirees who go away for long periods of time.

Subscriber Mix:

Foreign listings:	65%
USA listings:	35%

Foreign Listings Profile:

Most of the Loan-A-Home listings are abroad, mainly in the London area, with a large number also in France and Italy. While some 24 countries are represented in the directory listings of the current year, only a small number of these are found outside England, France and Italy.

USA Listings Profile:

Although roughly half of the states in the USA are represented, the domestic listings are found primarily in California, the New York City area, Pennsylvania, Massachusetts and Florida.

Club Strengths and Weaknesses:

Loan-A-Home is an established agency with a good track record. The club lists homes and apartments in cities, academic centers and resort areas throughout the world. This provides a useful clearing house service for their specialized clientele of academic, business and retired people who usually need long-term accommodations. Most of the opportunities exist for exchangers from the USA seeking exchanges or rentals abroad.

Rental opportunities probably outnumber the exchange opportunities. The majority of listings include a rental figure but do not indicate if an exchange is also available. The majority of the clients, the director indicates, rent at both ends, whether domestic or abroad.

Listing descriptions are brief with only minimal information about home amenities, the number of members in an exchange party, or exchanger profile.

Worldwide Home Exchange Club (Ltd.)

45 Hans Place
London SW1X 0JZ
England
Phone: (071) 589 6055

806 Brantford Avenue
Silver Spring, MD 20904
USA

Director:

M. J. Baer

Started:

1978

Size:

Worldwide Home Exchange directories carry 800-1,000 listings per year.

Subscription Fees: (annually)

Listed subscribers:	$20.00
Unlisted subscribers:	$18.00
Listing (second home):	$ 5.00
Optional photo:	$ 6.00

Directories:

Worldwide Home Exchange publishes two directories yearly —in January and April. January is the main directory with an additional supplement in April. Exchanges are listed in one directory or the other, depending upon when the subscription is received. Copies of both publications for the year are sent to all subscribers, regardless of when they join.

The directory contains 10 pages of detailed suggestions on how to go about arranging a home exchange— what to look for, insurance, and many other important considerations.

Types of Listings Included:

Listings include home exchange, hospitality exchange and rentals.

Exchanger Profile:

Responsible, seasoned travelers, mainly from the professional, educational and business worlds.

Subscriber Mix:

Foreign listings: 75%
USA listings: 25%

Foreign Listings Profile:

The listings include 38 countries, mainly European. About half of the listings abroad are in the United Kingdom, with a large concentration in Greater London.

The current year's directories show the following listings breakdown:

England, Scotland & Ireland	312
Continental Europe	166
Australia & New Zealand	67
Canada	36
Caribbean & Mexico	26

The club listings also include their share of out-of-the-way exchange offerings—Cyprus, Kenya, Malta, Solomon Islands, Syria and Zimbabwe.

Club representatives have been appointed recently in Czechoslovakia, Hungary and Singapore and expect to recruit more exchange candidates from these areas.

USA Listings Profile:

Total USA listings for the current year number about 200. These listings are found mainly in Florida (55 listings) and California (51 listings). However 35 of the states are represented in all.

Club Strengths and Weaknesses:

The subscriber ratio of mainly Europeans creates a favorable balance for Americans who wish to exchange abroad. Opportunities are most plentiful in England, especially the London area. The subscriber mix is more limited for foreign exchangers who seek an exchange in the USA.

With its 67 listings for Australia and New Zealand, Worldwide Exchange Club offers unique exchange possibilities in the now popular "Down Under" area.

5
Teachers' Home Exchange Clubs

Several of the larger home exchange clubs sprang up out of a teacher/educator membership base.

Intervac International began as a home exchange for teachers in Europe, but its clientele are now made up largely of other professions. Its teacher/educator subscribers currently make up an estimated one-third of the membership.

Likewise, the Vacation Exchange Club of the Directory Group Association first targeted teachers but early on began to aim its advertising efforts at professionals in general. Their current teacher/educator subscribers probably account for one-fourth of the membership.

Loan-A-Home exchange club has a mixed clientele that is oriented toward the academic and business world.

Aside from these there are a number of home exchange clubs in operation which cater to teachers/educators exclusively. While their services are provided for teachers/educators only, this service usually extends to adjunct faculty, part-time and substitute, as well as retired teachers/educators.

The clubs listed below provide good contacts if you are interested in "teachers only" home exchanges.

AFT NAS/UWT Home Exchange Program

555 New Jersey Avenue, NW
Washington, DC 20001
Phone: (202) 879-4400

NAS/UWT Home Exchange Program

Hillscourt Education Centre, Rednal
Birmingham B45 8RS
England

Director:

Karen D. Vines

Started:

1985

Size:

Currently the American branch (American Federation of Teachers) has about 40 participants. The English branch (National Association of Schoolmasters/Union of

Women Teachers of Great Britain) has about 22 participants.

Subscription Fees:

One-time enrollment fee: $25.00

Directories:

The AFT NAS/UWT Home Exchange publishes no directory as such. As applications from American subscribers are received, copies of the forms are sent to subscribers in England. Likewise, copies of applications from English subscribers are forwarded to their American counterparts.

Types of Listings:

Home exchange and reciprocal host family visits.

Exchanger Profile:

Teachers/educators, active or retired, who belong to the American Federation of Teachers or the NAS/UWT in England.

Subscriber Mix:

Foreign listings: 35%
USA listings: 65%

Foreign Listings Profile:

All participants must be union teacher/educators, active or retired. English enrollment is limited to members of the National Association of Schoolmasters/Union of Women Teachers of Great Britain.

Most of the NAS/UWT members are owner-occupants with family-size cars. Generally, their houses have three bedrooms and two living rooms with a garden.

USA Listings Profile:

American enrollment is limited to members of the American Federation of Teachers. Retired or inactive teachers may maintain an AFT membership-at-large for a yearly fee of $25.

Club Strengths and Weaknesses:

The AFT NAS/UWT Home Exchange Program offers an affordable opportunity for American AFT teachers to make friends with union counterparts in Great Britain, some 150,000 career-minded members. The currently small number of participants limits exchange options.

American participants complain that homes are not available for the time requested, or in the preferred areas of England. The majority of NAS/UWT members are located in Northern England. Instead of swapping homes, some members find it advantageous to host a family one year with the hosted family doing likewise the following year.

Faculty Exchange Center

952 Virginia Avenue
Lancaster, PA 17603
Phone: (717) 393-1130

Director:

John Joseph, Ph.D.

Started:

1973

Size:

The current year's directory shows 226 home exchange listings.

Subscription Fees: (annually)

Listing in teaching exchange directory:	$25.00
Listing in house exchange supplement:	$25.00
Listing in both directory & supplement:	$30.00

Directories:

The Faculty Exchange Center publishes a teaching exchange directory early in the fall. Deadline for inclusion in the directory is June 30. The directory indicates if faculty members are willing to exchange their houses.

In order to facilitate housing exchanges only during the summers, holidays and sabbatical leaves, the Center publishes a house exchange supplement, which is also distributed in early fall. The house exchange supplement is made available to all teachers and administrators at any level of the education profession.

Upon registration, you are mailed the current directory and/or supplement, whether your name made the publication deadline or not. This enables you to initiate correspondence immediately upon joining. Your name will be included in the directory and supplement of the following fall, which you also receive without extra payment. Upon request, the Center will also include your name in a future issue of its directories gratis if you have not been successful in your efforts to negotiate an exchange. All in all, the club provides quite a bit of service for the fee paid.

Types of Listings:

Faculty Exchange Center is a non-profit, faculty-administered program to facilitate the interchange of educators among campuses or in the exchange of homes. Listings include faculty exchange with house exchange, house exchange only. Participation in the faculty exchange is limited to higher education professionals. Participation in the house exchange only is limited to teachers and administrators at all levels of the education profession.

Listings in the directories usually indicate no dates for the exchange wanted. As a rule, it is understood that exchanges are for summers, holidays and sabbaticals.

Exchanger Profile:

All listed subscribers are teachers and/or administrators, mainly at the higher education level.

Subscriber Mix:

Foreign listings:	30%
USA listings:	70%

Foreign Listings Profile:

Listings for foreign countries have included Australia, Canada, Egypt, France, Greece, Hong Kong, India,

Ireland, Israel, New Guinea, New Zealand, Spain, Sweden and the United Kingdom. The current Supplement includes about 70 foreign listings representing 6 countries. Canada makes the strongest showing with 41 listings in 8 provinces. Australia and New Zealand follow with a total of 19 listings. The United Kingdom (5), Sweden (1) and Korea (1) are the other foreign countries represented.

USA Listings Profile:

In recent years members whose names have appeared in the Faculty Exchange Directory and Supplement have come from all parts of the United States including Alaska, the District of Columbia, Guam, Hawaii, Puerto Rico and the Virgin Islands. The current Supplement shows about 150 USA listings representing 20 states. Pennsylvania (FEC headquarters) indicates the most listings (25), followed by New York (24), California (24) and Tennessee (20).

Club Strengths and Weaknesses:

Faculty Exchange Center offers educators opportunity for home exchanges within their own profession with time-slots (summers, holidays and sabbaticals) that are likely to dove-tail.

The most opportunities exist for exchanges within the USA or for exchanges between Canadian and USA exchangers. Few overseas exchanges are available aside from the English-speaking countries. While Australia and New Zealand currently show the most listings abroad, the United Kingdom is more often the country with the most listings abroad.

Teacher Swap

P.O. Box 4130
Rocky Point, NY 11778
Phone: (516) 744-6403

Director:

Glenn Hameroff

Started:

1985

Size:

Teacher Swap has had about 1,000 subscribers since 1985. The directory and supplement for the current year show more than 400 listings.

Subscription Fees: (annually)

Listing in directory:	$34.00
Non-listed subscribers:	$40.00

Directories:

Teacher Swap publishes two directories each year— in March and May. The main directory is mailed in March followed by the May supplement, containing the names of subscribers enrolled between March 10 and May 1. Listings are grouped by regions of the USA with separate groupings for Canada, European and other foreign countries. Subscribers who list a European destination as one of their choices will have their listing published in the

French affiliate, Echanges Enseignants. Affiliates have also now been appointed in England, Germany and Spain.

Types of Listings:

Listings include home exchange only, exchange of bed-and-breakfast courtesies, or bed-and-breakfast offered for a fee negotiated between colleagues.

Exchanger Profile:

All listed subscribers are teacher/educators, including adjunct faculty, part-time and substitute, active and retired. The Echanges Enseignants also arranges student exchanges between the USA and Europe.

Subscriber Mix:

Foreign listings:	35%
USA listings:	65%

Foreign Listings Profile:

The current year's directories contain 415 listings with a third (137) of these abroad. Some 26 of these listings are from six Canadian provinces.

The international mix is improving with the recent addition of the French home exchange affiliate, Echanges Enseignants, as well as affiliates in England, Germany and Spain. Listings abroad include 12 foreign countries. France shows 70 listings and the German affiliate already has more than 100 listings in East Germany for the 1991 directory, many of whom have expressed interest in swapping homes with American and Canadian teachers.

The remainder of the foreign listings are from Australia, Bermuda, England, Finland, Ireland, Morocco, Norway, Republic of China, Romania, Scotland, Spain, the Virgin Islands and West Germany.

USA Listings Profile:

The majority of current Teacher Swap listings for the USA are located in California (54), followed by New York (50) and Florida (28).

Most of the subscribers, at home and abroad, list as their preference home exchange only or the home exchange/bed-and-breakfast option. A smaller number of bed-and-breakfast only preferences are indicated.

The bulk of the listings are, by far, primary residences. Secondary properties such as vacation homes are indicated in the directory by an asterisk (*) and a separate address for contact. About 10 percent of the current listings are designated as secondary properties available for exchange.

Club Strengths and Weaknesses:

Teacher Swap offers a specialized service for those teachers/educators (active or retired) who wish to exchange homes or offer bed-and-breakfast to others of the teaching profession. The club has grown rapidly since its beginning in 1985 and shows a solid base of subscribers.

With a subscriber mix of almost two to one in favor of domestic listings, Teacher Swap offers the most for those who wish to exchange within the USA. Likewise, more opportunities exist for the foreign teacher to exchange in the USA than for the American teacher to find an exchange abroad.

However, with the recent appointment of several European affiliates, this picture is rapidly changing. It appears that not only France but a good many other European countries such as Germany will now have a great deal to offer exchange candidates.

6
Full-Service Home Exchange Clubs

The full-service home exchange clubs are more personalized than the directory exchange clubs. The full-service exchange clubs do not publish directories; instead, they handle the details of home exchanging for you.

You send in an application, ordinarily with photographs of your home, indicate the dates wanted for a home exchange, and list other pertinent information about yourself and what you have to offer, as well as what you seek in exchange. The club then sets about to arrange a swap for you. Usually an application fee is required, with an additional charge made upon finalization of an exchange agreement. The total cost of a typical exchange customarily runs between $200 and $500, or more.

For this charge, the full-service clubs provide additional service and security. Through applicant screening, they attempt to make your exchange as successful as possible. Applicants are interviewed, prospective homes are inspected and personal references are required. Search is made for an exchange partner whose home is suitable to your vacation needs, and a description and photographs of your prospective exchange home and its facilities are supplied.

Usually, information and reservations on regularly scheduled flights and charter flights are included in the service, as well as, an optional vacation insurance plan. Practical suggestions for a successful exchange, including travel tips and itineraries, may also come as part of the package. For those home exchangers who like to leave the details of exchange arrangements to someone else, this may be the way to go.

Full-service home exchange clubs generally have not fared well in comparison with the directory clubs. The attrition rate has been high with more than one of these clubs having recently ceased operation or modified its operation. (The Great Exchange Ltd. and Global Home Exchange & Travel Service, for instance.) Home Exchange International has modified its approach and now operates as a combination home exchange and travel service under the new name, Better Homes and Travel.

If your interest lies in a home exchange club through which a more trouble-free (and expensive) exchange can be made, contact one of these full-service clubs.

Better Homes and Travel

P.O. Box 268
New York, NY 10272
Phone: (212) 349-5340
FAX: (212) 608-2338

22713 Ventura Boulevard, Suite F
Woodland Hills, CA 91364
Phone: (818) 992-8990

Director:

Linda McCall

Started:

1985

Size:

Better Homes and Travel, under its prior name of Home
Exchange International, has customarily run about 500
subscribers per year. Due to problems with its overseas
representatives, the club has recently experienced a drop
in placements. They now have new representatives,
however, and the situation should improve, according to
the assistant director.

Subscription Fees:

Lifetime registration fee:	$50.00
Closing fee:	$150.00 to $525.00

The closing fee depends upon the type of home,
whether the swap is domestic or international, and the
length of the swap and period of exchange.

Types of Listings:

Listings include primary residences and vacation
properties.

Subscriber Mix:

Foreign listings: 50%
USA listings: 50%

Most of the listing strength is in the USA, France, Italy and England, with representatives in these respective countries. Representatives are being recruited for Portugal, Spain and Switzerland.

Club Strengths and Weaknesses:

Better Homes and Travel has been in operation since 1985 under its prior name of Home Exchange International and is one of the survivors of the full-service exchange group. Better Homes and Travel offers a total service for home exchangers, including long and short-term exchanges in the USA and abroad. The club helps arrange for peripheral services such as competitive travel rates, bed-and-breakfast accommodations, sightseeing and side trips, which create a total vacation package. The club attempts to match lifestyles as well as homes.

The club offers opportunities for those who wish a home exchange arranged in England, France and Italy primarily, or for subscribers from those countries who would like an exchange in the USA. Recruiting efforts indicate more offerings to be expected soon from Portugal and Spain.

Homeshare Holidays

3 Main Street
New Elgin, Elgin
Moray, IV30 3BQ
United Kingdom
Phone: (0343) 482118 (24 hours)

Director:

Phil Hadfield

Started:

1988

Subscription Fees:

Per overseas exchange:	55 pounds
Disabled clients:	50 pounds
There is no registration fee.	

Types of Listings:

Listings include home exchanges. Homeshare Holidays places special emphasis upon accommodations for the disabled.

Club Strengths and Weaknesses:

Homeshare Holidays provides a special service to the disabled exchanger. Disabled clients benefit from the increased opportunity to vacation in suitably adapted accommodations.

Homeshare Holidays is registered with all the large disabled organizations in the United Kingdom and a few overseas. They are also registered with the British Tourist Authority in London and Edinburgh. They can arrange travel and insurance for disabled clients through the Assistance Travel Service in England who specialize in travel for the disabled. They are also approved and recommended by the International Disabled Travellers Club.

The club is relatively new and offers limited exchange opportunities at present, mainly in the United Kingdom. Potential for an increased and expanded subscriber base is indicated.

7
Time-Share Vacation Exchanges

Time-share resort networks, with their thousands of vacation properties, offer still other options for the prospective home exchanger. Restrictions may apply and ownership of time-share property is usually required. However, within these networks, abundant vacation home exchange opportunities are available to the non-owner of resort property, if he only knows where to inquire.

These are sources to contact about time-share vacation exchanges.

Interval International

6262 Sunset Drive
Miami, FL 33143
Phone: (305) 666-1861

Service Offered:

Through their Computrade computer network, Interval International offers a variety of time-share vacation exchange options for their membership.

Subscription Fees: (annually)

Individual membership fee: $54.00
Exchange fee for each week: $64.00

Restrictions:

Membership is limited to owners of resort property. In addition, the resort must belong to the Interval International network.

Strengths and Weaknesses:

Interval International includes in its membership hundreds of quality resorts in over 35 countries around the world. This opens almost unlimited vacation exchange destinations for those who qualify.

Their main limitation is that only time-share owners who own property in a resort that belongs to the Interval International network can qualify for the exchange service.

Intrex Exchange Network

27 Hyland Road
P.O. Box 436
Depew, NY 14043
Phone: 1-800-872-5277

Service Offered:

Intrex bills itself as the Master Exchange Company for time-share owners. Intrex is able to cut across the resort membership requirements of such networks as Interval International and Resort Condominiums International so that non-owners of resort property can qualify for vacation time-share exchanges.

Although some resorts have stringent contracts with exchange networks, the individual time-share owners in these resorts do not. They are free to exchange with whomever they wish. Intrex listings come from these time-share owners, which offers exchanges into resorts that were previously unavailable to you. (Intrex has replaced the Exchange Network—Ocean Springs, MS.— with its extensive computerized base of individual time-share owners who wish to exchange.)

Intrex will list your home if you have a desirable primary residence or vacation property. Send your request to the attention: Virginia Scheeler, Vice-President of Operations. Include pictures of your property, a list of amenities, why your location is desirable, and the time slot desired. They do the rest.

Subscription Fees:

First year enrollment:	$99.00
If you own at affiliated resort:	$75.00
Seniors get a 10% discount.	
Annual renewal fee:	$49.00
Exchange fee (per week):	
Within home resort:	$55.00
Within North America:	$65.00
Intercontinental:	$85.00

Restrictions:

There is no membership requirement that exchangers own time-share property. Participation is not limited to resorts that belong to a network since exchanges are done through individual subscribers.

Strengths and Weaknesses:

Intrex furnishes a time-share service that gives property owners exchange options at over 700 resorts worldwide. Time-share owners from any resort may participate as individuals, regardless of their resort affiliation. Home owners who are non-owners of resort property may also list with Intrex.

Subscribers receive a Resort Directory that is the largest in the time-share industry. It contains information on accommodations and amenities at the resorts.

Resort Condominiums International

P.O. Box 80229
Indianapolis, IN 46280-0229
Phone: (317) 846-4727
Enrollment hotline: (800) 338-7799

Service Offered:

Resort Condominiums International compiles a data bank of time-share owners who wish to exchange their vacation property time with another time-share owner at another resort. Either RCI or the owner arranges the exchange after prospects are matched up.

Subscription Fees:

Exchange fee for each week requested:

Within home resort:	$ 59.00
Within USA or Canada:	$ 84.00
Intercontinental:	$109.00

Restrictions:

The exchanger must own resort property, and the resort must belong to the Resort Condominiums International network.

Strengths and Weaknesses:

Resort Condominiums International is the largest and oldest time-share exchange network in the world. RCI offers you more than 1,500 member resorts in 50 countries with more than 950,000 families participating. This gives practically unlimited vacation exchange potential world-wide if you own property in a desirable location, have a tempting time-slot, and your resort is a member of the RCI network. RCI says they helped more than 495,000 people with exchange vacations last year.

Exchanges are limited to those with other RCI locations, and prospective exchangers who do not own time-share property in an RCI affiliate resort are not eligible. RCI publishes the monthly magazine, Endless Vacation, which you can subscribe to by calling the hotline.

8
How Do I Make A Vacation Home Exchange?

The first step in making a successful vacation home exchange is to join the exchange club (or clubs) that is right for you. This will get your listing into their club directory, let other exchange candidates know what you have to offer and what you want, and give you access to their listings.

As indicated earlier, it is possible to find a vacation home exchange without belonging to an exchange club, by going it on your own. You can run an ad in a newspaper of the area where you wish to exchange. You can advertise in a magazine or newsletter that reaches a particular audience of potential exchangers. However, most vacation home exchanges are arranged through listings in club directories, so stick with them. Any other approach, except in specialized situations, greatly limits your chances of finding the exchange you want.

Club profiles contained in the preceding chapters provide information that will help you in making the right choice of club or clubs. Review the club strengths and weaknesses, the extent and location of their listings, their specialties and special services, and you will have a good basis for making an informed choice when you put your money down.

What About My Listing?

You can subscribe to an exchange club and get access to the listings in their directories without listing your own property. This is not, as a rule, a good idea unless you are only window-shopping. Without a listing in the directory, no one will know of your interests and you will get no contacts from potential exchangers. If unlisted, you must take all the initiative for finding an exchange.

It is important to get your listing in the main directory of the club you join. Most of the clubs publish their main directories in the late winter or early spring. One or more supplements usually follow later in the spring or even into the fall. Your chances of finding an exchange are best if you get into the club's main directory. The bulk of their listings, and sometimes the best ones, show up in the main directory, so get going early with your listing. If you fail to make the deadline for the club's main directory, however, do not hesitate to use the later supplements as many of them offer excellent listings.

Your listing will include pertinent information about your exchange offer and the exchange that you desire.

Your name, address and phone number go into the listing so interested parties can make direct contact. The exchange club is only a middle-man that by and large steps out of the picture after the directory of listings is published. From there on, the responsibility and the fun of making a successful exchange is left up to you. In reality, however, the directory clubs often do step in to assist in last-minute or emergency situations where an exchange has fallen through or has not yet been arranged.

Your listing will usually describe the number of adults and children in your party, describe your home with its amenities, and indicate the areas of exchange preferred, also if a car is offered in the exchange.

The most important thing in your listing is location. California, Florida and Hawaii are favorites with exchangers. San Francisco, coastal resort areas, Los Angeles with its proximity to Disneyland, or Orlando, Florida with its Disney World, are favorite localities. Remember, the vacation home exchanger more often than not plans to use your home as a base for sight-seeing excursions, be they short or long. As a rule, he is more interested in where your home is located or what interesting place it is located near, or at least within driving distance of, than he is in your home's special amenities.

So this is the thing to emphasize in your listing. If you are located near Yosemite National Park, say so. If salmon fishing is great this time of year on the Rogue River, situated almost at your back door, announce it. Whether your home has a barbecue, microwave, CD player, washer and dryer and central heating is of lesser importance. The average home exchanger does not plan to spend his vacation sitting in your home, no matter how nice the amenities. Where listing space in the directory does not allow for such information, at least get the word out on what you have to offer when you make contact with a potential exchanger.

Location usually becomes more important to the exchange candidate than finding a home that is equal in value or accommodations to his own. Your condo in Hawaii may fetch a two-week stay in a palatial villa in Spain with no questions asked. It depends upon what the exchanger places as top priority in his exchange. Sometimes that priority is for seclusion and serenity away from it all in a remote fishing lodge or other Canadian hideaway. If that is the exchanger's desire, then your vacation property in British Columbia may go for a high-price on the exchange auction block.

DON'T BE AFRAID TO TOUT WHAT YOU HAVE TO OFFER. DON'T BE RELUCTANT TO ASK FOR WHAT YOU WANT IN EXCHANGE.

The most important thing about your listing, after location, is your flexibility. If you must have Oberammergau the last two weeks of the Passion Play, you have severely restricted your chances, unless you started ten years earlier, perhaps. Leave your time slots and area choices as open as possible. Who knows, you may get an offer that is better than what you originally had in mind? And if that first choice for an exchange is taken this year, check out the possibilities of arranging that same exchange for the next year.

How Do I Make A Home Exchange Proposal?

When you subscribe to a vacation home exchange club, pay the few extra dollars for your directory to come air mail, unless this is automatically included in the fee.

Some directories are printed and shipped from abroad. Early delivery will give you the jump on contacting those exchangers who look interesting. More than one exchanger says he picks up the phone and calls the minute he spots a desirable exchange. If both parties are interested in what the other has to offer, follow-up can be done by mail. The best offers will go first. By taking the initiative, you improve your chances of getting first in line. The last approach to use is to sit back passively and wait for offers.

Don't be afraid to contact someone who has not expressed a preference for your particular area. There are usually not enough first preferences for everybody. Most exchangers are willing to consider second or third choices, or even locations they never thought of before. Often any resemblance between an initially stated preference and the actual exchange that is eventually made is purely coincidental.

If you do not use the phone approach, at least have a form letter ready for mailing when the directory arrives. The more proposal letters mailed, the more chances you have of getting the right exchange. Some exchangers mail thirty or forty or more letters.

The letter should include the brief basics of what you have to offer and the details of importance to your exchange. How many are in your party? What are the ages of the children? What dates do you wish and what is the length of stay desired? How flexible are you? Give a description of your home and area. List local attractions. Indicate your profession/occupation and personal interests. If a car exchange is available, include that. Sell the prospect by telling him what he will enjoy about your home and area. All of this information may be set down on a separate information sheet to be accompanied by a short personal cover letter, if you prefer.

Some exchangers send stamped, self-addressed return envelopes in their contacts. With letters going abroad, they include International Reply Coupons. Experienced exchangers find that this is not necessary. If your offer is inviting, you can depend upon the potential exchanger to respond, franking fees notwithstanding, for exchanges do not hinge upon the price of a postage stamp. At best, self-addressed, stamped envelopes may encourage more responses—in the form of a courteous "no."

While you await answers to your mailings, other exchange offers may come. Give each inquirer the courtesy of answering his letter, even though the answer may be "no." Indicate to him if there is the possibility of an exchange at a later date, and keep a file of these contacts for possible future contact. Likewise, some of the proposals you send out may come back negative, but with indications of a likely future exchange arrangement.

You may get offers that are not exactly on target for your desired exchange. Here, again, flexibility is important. Remember, for instance, that all of Europe is comparatively small, about the size of Texas and California combined. Paris may be your first choice, but it is only a few hours drive from Brussels or major cities in Austria, southern Germany, or northern Italy.

Expect that some exchangers will not reply. Exchangers living in the more popular areas of London, Paris, Rome, Florida and California often receive more offers than they can handle. Take another look at the directory and continue with more contacts.

How Do I Arrange An Exchange?

After the initial sending out of exchange proposals, your next step is to sort through the most attractive offers that come in. At this point, you begin in-depth contact with the would-be exchanger. Some exchanges have been arranged with one or two phone calls, but most exchangers are not this lucky. More phone calls and letters usually follow, to supply additional information, answer needful questions and iron out all the other details.

Once the two parties make a commitment to exchange, and the dates are decided on, this agreement should remain firm. Breaking an exchange agreement because a better offer comes along is taboo among home exchangers. Broken commitments, though rare, can cause serious inconvenience to the other party, especially when air fares have been paid for and are non-refundable. If an emergency demands that you break an agreement, try to make it mutually agreeable or at least palatable. Look for an alternate for the exchanger, try to arrange a different time, or contact the exchange club about last-minute suggestions and assistance.

Most exchangers get to know each other quite well before the actual exchange takes place. You will want to swap detailed information about your respective homes and the people who live in them, as well as the surrounding areas.

Sending An Exchange Packet

In the process of getting ready for the exchange, prospective home exchangers will find it a good idea to send packets to each other to include the following items and information.

Photographs

Photographs will include members of the exchange party, as well as shots of the exterior and interior of the home, and the car.

Description of the Home

Be completely honest. Stress all the good features of your home but do not overstate its advantages. Is part of your home occupied by someone else? Is the property primarily a rental? What is the floor plan and accessibility, especially if multi-level? What are the amenities?

Description of Surrounding Areas

How accessible are public transportation, shopping, recreational facilities? Be specific rather than talk in general terms that are subject to misinterpretation. Does "walking distance" mean three blocks or three miles?

Exchange References

If your exchange partner is an experienced home exchanger, your best reference will come from one of his prior exchange partners. This may take the form of a short letter of personal reference, or you may telephone the prior exchange partner. References from other personal and business sources are not that valid. They may not be all that familiar with the exchanger or his home.

Packets on Your Local Areas

These should include maps, travel folders and tourist guide books. Such materials can be obtained from national, state and local tourist offices or chambers of commerce. These offices will usually mail packets directly to your exchange partners upon request, thus saving you the packaging effort and mailing costs. Many of these offices have "800" numbers so that your requests can be handled free of phone call charges or even the bother of a letter. You should do your exchanger the courtesy of having these materials sent to him so he can begin to familiarize himself with your area before setting off. At the very least, leave the materials at your home if they are not sent ahead of time. Materials that you especially want to leave for your exchanger are materials having to do with things not in the guide books.

You can also request your own materials for almost any country that you plan to visit abroad via a simple phone call to one of their offices located in the USA. Most of the Canadian provincial tourist offices can be contacted from the USA with an "800" number. See the book sections on national, state and local tourist offices for helpful addresses and phone numbers.

Having done the things discussed above, you will have step one out of the way toward preparing for your home exchange adventure. At this point, you are almost certain to have a good many questions about the details of your home exchange. Your next step is to bring up these questions, clarify, and reach mutual agreement on the many items that are important to the success of your exchange. These items are discussed in the following chapter.

9
What Do Exchangers Need To Agree Upon?

Don't hesitate to ask questions, dispel doubts and clear up crucial points during the arranging of a home exchange. This is the time to do it, not after you and the exchanger are in each other's home. It is impossible to exchange homes without having some kind of mutual expectations, responsibilities and agreements in mind. Yours may not always coincide with those of your exchange partner unless they are expressed ahead of time.

A signed letter of agreement or contract is not worth much because it is unenforceable. Most home exchangers come to mutual agreement on their expectations via phone calls and letters which cover what they consider important to their home swap. While this may transpire rather casually, a final written summary of what has been agreed upon is a good idea. Such a summary will help to clarify issues as well as to remind each party of his or her responsibilities.

The summary can take the form of an exchange agreement, if that makes you feel more comfortable. Or, just as effectively, it can go out in a regular letter to the exchanger as a recap of what you have agreed upon. In either instance, the exchanger may delete, change or add to anything in the summary, initial the changes, and return it to the sender.

If neither of these approaches appeals to you, you may simply want to leave such a summary agreement in your home to indicate your expectations of the exchanger. A structured checklist or booklet containing this summary, as well as other relevant information for your exchanger, is probably a better idea. You must decide which approach you prefer.

Spoken, written or merely mutually understood, agreement upon certain significant items is essential for a successful home exchange. The following important items are some that you will not want to overlook in the rush of excitement to get on with your house-swapping adventure.

How Many Are In the Exchange Party?

Be up-front about the number of people in your party and determine the size of your exchange partner's group. If your entourage includes children, say so and state their ages. It is only honest to inform the exchanger if you expect guests while in his home and to get his permission. You want to avoid the surprise of last-minute complimentary kids or cousins. If your directory listing indicates "non-smokers," clarify that members of the exchanger's party are non-smokers. so you will not arrive at your destination to find a smoke-filled home.

How Firm Are the Exchange Dates?

Verify the dates of the exchange. It is a good idea to do a follow-up check before the exchange date arrives to see if everything is still "go." Determine if there are any extenuating circumstances which might necessitate cutting short the exchange— business obligations, etc. Decide on a contingency plan if this is likely to occur. If you have to return home early, will you find hotel accommodations, for instance?

What About Transportation From the Airport?

Where possible, it is desirable for one of the exchangers to meet the other at the airport, although this does not usually occur. Overlapping departures and arrivals can make this possible. If it is convenient, you can delay your departure to meet your guest at a designated point in the airport.

If you do this, remain aware of international time zones and the International Date Line so that you do not show up at an incorrect hour or even on the wrong day. You can plan to meet your exchange party at the airport, turn your car over to them, give them the house keys and receive theirs, and then take your flight of departure shortly afterwards. There is only one problem here. Your exchange partner's flight may not arrive on time, nor in time for you to catch your flight. Should this occur you will be left holding either your bags for a later departure or, if you depart on time, their keys to your car and home. Save such split-second timing for another occasion. A better alternative is to meet your guests at the airport on one day and take your flight out the following day.

The usual procedure for transportation from the airport is for both parties to make arrangements with a friend or family member to meet the exchange party at the airport and drive them to the host home. If this is not possible, clear instructions for public transportation and directions to the host home should be given. Likewise, instructions for key pickup or arrangements for access to the host home will be necessary.

Who Pays the Utility Bills?

It is customary for the owner of the home to pay utility bills except for phone calls, with each party paying his own toll calls. Charges for long-distance calls may be obtained from the operator and the appropriate amount of money left behind for the host. You may not be able to obtain such charges from the operator in some countries, England for instance, and will need to determine the amount owed later.

What About Yard and Garden Care?

As with any vacation, the home owner should arrange for his yard and pool care so as not to burden the guests.

What About Cleaning Help?

The home owner usually takes the responsibility of retaining and paying for any regular cleaning help. If the guest exchanger hires a maid, payment becomes his responsibility.

What About Household Pets?

Pets should not be left to the responsibility of the guests unless special arrangements have been agreed upon ahead of time. Since exchangers ordinarily use the host home as a base for sight-seeing trips, they do not want to be tied down with pet care. If this is important to you, clarify ahead of time to avoid a gratuitous cat or dog.

What About Damage In the Home?

It is the responsibility of the one causing the damage to have it repaired or pay for it.

What About Appliance Repairs?

Agree ahead of time about appliance, plumbing and other household repairs. If necessary repairs are to cost above a given figure, you may want the guest to call you, where possible, to insure that you agree to the repairs. If emergency situations arise, the guest should have instructions about what to do.

How Does Home Insurance Work?

In general, home insurance is in effect up to thirty days of guest occupancy. However, if the guest is paying rent or other remuneration, you will probably need additional rental coverage to insure against fire, theft, breakage and vandalism. If the guest will be there for a long stay, of thirty days or more, this may make a difference also. Check with your insurance agent.

What About A Car Exchange?

If your exchange partner's listing in the Vacation Exchange Club directory or the Intervac International directory, for instance, carries the "ae" code, that is a plus. You have hit upon a home exchanger who also wants an "auto exchange." Next to getting the right location in your exchange, being able to get around and see things is the top priority with home exchangers, more so than luxurious accommodations. For this reason, car exchanges along with home exchanges have become more and more common.

Few problems related to car exchanges are reported, and you should arrange one if you can, unless you prefer not to drive in the host country. It is much cheaper to exchange cars than to go with a high-priced rental, and the car exchange, as a rule, is preferable to public transportation for both cost and convenience. Practically your only transportation expense is for gasoline. Your car exchange makes an attractive offer for the European exchanger coming to the USA because of cheap gas prices compared with those in Europe.

If you do decide to exchange cars, certain agreements and considerations are in order. These are some of the important items to cover.

Car Condition

The condition of the car is your key item. The car should be tuned up and not in need of major repairs. Exchangers should indicate the make and year of their car or cars, for sometimes more than one vehicle is offered in an exchange. However, the condition of the car and its adequacy of size for the exchange party is probably of more importance than the year and make. Leave your car clean, filled with gas and a recent oil change. Leave operating instructions and an extra set of car keys, as well as another set of keys for a third party friend or family member. The user of the car is responsible for routine maintenance but not for repairs that would have been needed anyway. Agree ahead of time how such repairs, if needed, are to be taken care of.

Insurance

Generally, home and/or car insurance will be in force for thirty days no matter who is using the home or the car, but you should not take this for granted. Check with your insurance agent to make sure. Determine from your exchange partner if you are fully insured for liability and property damage while operating his automobile. Your own policy should fully cover any car you drive domestically with the permission of the owner. However, your policy at home probably will not cover you for all European driving. In the event of accident, it is customary that the operator of each vehicle is liable for the deductible ($100 -$500 usually) of the insurance policy if he is at fault.

Driving Restrictions

Set up any restrictions you feel necessary related to the use of your vehicle so that nothing in this respect is left to guesswork. You will want to consider the following.

Drivers— Indicate if you restrict drivers of your car to those over age 25.

Mileage— Agree upon the maximum distances or total miles that your vehicle will be driven.

Off-Limit Areas— Indicate if you do not wish your car driven out of state or out of the country. You will need a special certificate of insurance from your agent when driving into Canada, if involved in an accident. If your car is driven into Mexico, only insurance written by a Mexican insurance company is valid. Short of this insurance, your car if involved in an accident in Mexico can be held, as can the driver himself, until settlement is made. And a non-owner of your vehicle who drives it into Mexico and is stopped for registration check can find both himself and the vehicle impounded.

Driving Abroad— In Western Europe your USA or Canadian driver license will be accepted. Some East European countries will accept your license but others will not. You can play safe by acquiring an International Driving Permit. Obtain this permit at the AAA or the National Automobile Club, among others, for a few dollars whether you are a member of these clubs or not. The International Driving Permit is not available in Europe.

The items discussed in this chapter are important to the safety and peace of mind of both you and your exchange party. Once they are agreed upon, you will be ready to move on to the next step in your home exchange venture—preparing your home for the exchanger.

10
How Do I Prepare My Home For the Exchange?

As part of the final preparations for the exchange party's stay in your home, you will want to consider some or all of the following things—preparing the home itself, making some social arrangements for your guests, laying out a checklist of helpful information and instructions, and leaving behind a welcome packet of useful materials. Attention to these final details will make your guests more comfortable and give you the satisfaction of knowing that all the important bases have been covered.

Prepare the Home Itself

Prepare your home for the exchange guests as you would for any other special guests. Make sure that the home is clean and neat and ready when they arrive. Ideally, your home will reflect to the exchangers the actual picture you have presented through your mail and phone contacts. Though housekeeping standards are relative from one individual to another, enough questions should have been asked by now that neither party is in for any unpleasant surprises. Exchanged photographs of the interior and exterior of your homes will give good indications of what to expect in accommodations and housekeeping standards.

Differences in levels of housekeeping, rather than theft or damage, are one of the few complaints voiced by home exchangers. What is neat and squeaky clean to one individual is not necessarily so to another. You must be flexible enough to allow for a certain amount of acceptance. It may turn out that your guests are the better housekeepers and will need to exercise some acceptance on their part.

Provide the necessary towels and linens for your guests to get off to a good start. Set aside plenty of closet and drawer space so they can unpack. This does not mean you have to clean out closets for an exchange of limited length. Most travelers carry few clothes, and a small section of a closet is usually adequate.

Make sure the refrigerator is cleaned out, except for staples. It should have enough food and beverages so that your guests do not have to rush out to a supermarket upon arrival. Leave a supply of staples in the pantry. As a rule, however, arranged dinner invitations with friends are best avoided the first night. Give your guests a chance to settle in.

Irreplaceable antiques and personal items should be stored away if there is concern about breakage, the more so where small children are involved. Lock up or store any papers, journals and personal records you want kept private, and do not hesitate to set up house rules. Indicate those items you wish used with care or not at all, perhaps your prized computer or sports equipment. Mention if any parts of the home are off-limits.

If children are involved in the exchange, you will want to remove harmful substances from the bathroom cabinets and from under the kitchen sink or elsewhere. Also store away any other items or equipment that might be harmful.

Make Some Social Arrangements For Your Guests

It is usually appreciated if you make arrangements for friends and neighbors to provide your guests hospitality during their stay, unless they have requested otherwise. Frequently, the dinners, sightseeing trips and participation in community life provided through friendly hosts become the highlight of the trip. The hosts may even enjoy these hospitality gestures more than the exchangers. Often friendships established through these contacts continue and the host and your guests later set up their own home exchanges.

And do not forget the "guest privileges" to be arranged, if any. You may want to make arrangements for your visitors to use your private club, to attend some special events, or to obtain certain hard-to-get tickets for a favorite show.

Leave A Checklist

Since misunderstandings can occur if you rely on verbal agreement alone, both parties should set down briefly their agreements and necessary instructions in a simple checklist that is left behind.

A checklist has the advantage that it covers dozens of little details that might get overlooked. More so, it collects in one easily accessible place all the miscellanea such as names of contacts, phone numbers and other items to make them more readily usable. Most of the items, no doubt, will have been covered already in you mail and phone contacts, but the checklist serves to fill in the gaps, to remind and to reinforce what has perhaps already been said.

Draw up one of your own making and leave it behind in a loose-leaf binder or notebook for your guests. If you send a blank copy to your exchange party ahead of time, they can complete a similar checklist and leave it behind to make your stay in their home go off better.

Whatever form your checklist takes, it should cover the following areas. You may think of others you want to add.

Exchange Agreements

Arrangements for yard, garden and pool maintenance.
Payment of telephone bills.
Any special arrangements for transportation to the airport.
Any contingency plans involved.

95

Arrangements for pet care.
Car exchange agreement: maintenance, driving restrictions, insurance, payment for damage.

Names and Telephone Numbers

Contacts
Primary person, neighbors and friends.
Person to call in an emergency.
Person designated for house or pet care in your absence.
People who wish to host your guests.

Emergency Telephone Numbers
Doctors, hospitals, police, fire department, house and car insurance agents.

Repair Services
Car, appliance, plumber, electrician, emergency road service.

Recreation and Entertainment
Restaurants, golf courses, theaters.

Special Instructions

Household Appliances
Instructions and manuals.
Burglar alarm, TV, VCR, air conditioning.

Car Operation
Instructions and manuals.
Items for special attention: oil, fuel, operation.

Household Maintenance

Chores and responsible person.
Care of house plants, pets, pool service, garbage pickup, breaker box location, water main cut-off.

Mail and Bills
Designated person or instructions.

Completion of an adequate checklist to cover the above nuts and bolts of home exchanging will make for a smoother, more enjoyable experience for both you and your exchange partners.

Leave A Welcome Packet

Add to your guests' welcome by leaving a packet of materials that they are certain to find interesting and useful. Some of these materials may have been forwarded already, but another fresh, more complete, packet left in your home ready for their use will be appreciated. These are some of the things you will want to include.

Local Tourist Packet

A tourist packet from the local Chamber of Commerce or Visitor's Bureau will provide maps, brochures and other information about tourist attractions and places of interest in your vicinity. You can use the maps to mark locations and routes for your guests to such places as the market, shopping center, or sites of interest.

Tourist Packets From Other Areas

You may also want to obtain tourist packets from the Visitor Bureaus of other areas or cities that your guests plan to visit. In practically every USA city of any size, a hometown expert known as the Convention and Visitor Bureau exists to make your visit or your exchange partner's visit easier. Aside from maps and brochures, their free services also include lists of major attractions and entertainment, calendars of events, restaurant guides and lodging accommodations.

Packets From State Tourist Offices

Each state has its own Office of Tourism which will gladly mail packets to you or your exchange partner abroad. A simple phone call handles all the details in a few moments, and the state Office of Tourism often has an "800" number, as do most of the Canadian provincial tourist offices.

Many of the state offices have excellent additional publications they will send if you ask for them. "Discover California" is a 192-page booklet for the visitor coming to California. The state of Washington offers a 196-page state travelers' guide, "Destination Washington." And Texas provides upon request a 248-page tourist book entitled "Texas." Ask if special publications are available.

Travel Books and Guides

You may also want to leave your guests other travel books and guides on their areas of interest. Dining out in San Francisco, special tours, independent travel tips, bed-and-breakfast accommodations are all likely items.

And you will want to include in your collection a courtesy copy of *The Vacation Home Exchange and Hospitality Guide* for your guests to take back home. Its useful information will make their arranging of that next home exchange even more enjoyable.

Once these details are out of the way, you and your exchange partner are ready to get on with a great adventure in hospitality sharing—the sharing of homes, community, cars and perhaps lifestyles.

11
Hospitality Exchanges

Hospitality exchanges offer an alternative to the vacation home exchange. A hospitality exchange club amounts to a network of friendly, travel-oriented people who provide each other hospitality in their homes. You offer a spare room or bed to travelers for a short stay when they come to your city. In return, they or other members of the network will usually do the same for you when you visit theirs.

Unlike a typical bed-and-breakfast or farmstay, where the traveler is strictly a paying guest, hospitality exchanges involve little or no exchange of money. Club membership, which gets your name into a directory, is required if you want to participate.

The hospitality exchange comes in several variations. Usually the exchange is round-robin rather than one-to-one. You offer hospitality to someone in your home, and someone else does the same for you. As a rule, the stay is short-term of one or two days. But there are no set rules. The exchange may, if you wish, consist of a reciprocal stay, where you spend a week or more with a family this summer and they return the visit the next summer. Or the hospitality may just as easily go on unilaterally with no expectation of an exchange.

As you get into hospitality stays, many options quickly enter the picture. The possibilities are almost endless, and you create them, or they create themselves, as you go along. Members of the home exchange clubs often find that when a home exchange cannot be arranged to fit their schedules they are offered a hospitality stay in the other member's home.

The hospitality stay is like visiting among relatives whose network is worldwide. It is especially appealing to those travelers who like the closer, one-on-one contact with people. For those who enjoy making new, perhaps lifelong, friendships, this approach to travel offers an inviting option.

How do you go about arranging a hospitality stay? The whole process is simple and informal. Unlike a home exchange, next to nothing is required in the way of planning or dove-tailing of schedules. Unless you want to join several short stays together into a marathon vacation venture, that is. That is possible, too. You just substitute hospitality stays for hotels and motels and, of course, knock off most of the lodging tab.

To participate in this type of exchanging, join one of the clubs, or several, of your choice. The small fees give you access to a directory of subscribers and get your listing into the directory. From there on, when planning your vacation, you merely call or write in advance to members in the directory located where you would like to stay. Arrangements are made for the number of nights you wish lodging, and that is it. Do not show up on the member's doorstep unannounced. Such visits are unappreciated and carry no obligation for accommodations.

With the hospitality exchange, it is common for members to offer their guests added amenities to include extended stays, meals, tours or other hospitality gestures. These should not be expected unless they are spelled out ahead of time.

Remember, too, that hosts are not obligated to honor requests for hospitality if the circumstances are inconvenient. Your listing in a directory means only that you intend to offer hospitality.

Any number of opportunities exist, even in the home exchange clubs, for those travelers who wish to arrange these family-like stays. Take a look at the directories of the home exchange clubs already discussed such as Vacation Exchange Club, Intervac International, Teacher Swap and Worldwide Home Exchange Club. A quick glance at their listings will turn up a great many hospitality stay and/or bed-and-breakfast offerings.

In addition to the home exchange clubs, more and more clubs that specialize solely in the hospitality stay are becoming available to the traveler. The following clubs are some to check out. If you decide the hospitality exchange is the way for you, and you have the space and willingness to welcome other travelers into your home, one or more of these clubs may offer just what you are looking for.

Globetrotters Club

BCM/Roving
London WC1N 3XX
England

Director:

Malcolm Keir

Started:

Started in 1947, Globetrotters is the oldest travel club of its kind in the world.

Size:

The membership is 1,500 worldwide.

Subscription Fees:

Joining/rejoining fee:	$ 5
1-year subscription:	$14
2-year subscription:	$24
3-year subscription:	$34

Subscriptions cover two people at the same address or traveling together. Subscriptions run for a calendar year.

Directories:

Members are sent a list of members from their own continental area. Lists of members from the other 3 continental areas cost $2 each. Listings include the profession/occupation and age bracket of the individual.

Globetrotters also publishes a bi-monthly magazine, Globe, that places emphasis on methods of cheap travel and trips off the beaten track. It also contains tips on what to watch for in foreign travel, information you do not get from the travel agent or embassy.

Types of Listings:

Members indicate the type of hospitality they will offer to fellow Globetrotters. A member may choose to offer one or all of the following: (1) advice on their country or area, (2) to welcome and show the guest the area, (3) accommodation for a night or two if given plenty of notice. While Globetrotters is not intended primarily to provide lodging for travelers, most members do in fact offer all three of the above options. Accommodations include beds and floor space.

As a member you can place a free ad in the club magazine: swap your camper van, exchange your house, find some like-minded companion for your trip.

Exchanger Profile:

The professions and occupations of the membership in-clude practically any specialty you can name. Teachers show up most frequently among the listings, with student listings next in frequency.

The age category 25-35 makes up about half of the listings. The 36-45 age category accounts for roughly a quarter of the listings.

Subscriber Mix:

Continental Europe - This group shows about 100 listings in the current directory. Twenty-one of the European countries are represented.

Africa, Middle East, Asia & Australia - This list accounts for the smallest group of members. While at least 20 countries are included, Australia and New Zealand combined register almost half of the listings.

USA - Listings in the current directory number about 300

United Kingdom - More than half of the club membership is located in the United Kingdom per the current directories.

Club Strengths and Weaknesses:

Globetrotters provides a loose network of members around the world who share common interests of independent, often adventurous, travel. These members offer free contacts, advice and helpful travel tips that might be difficult to come by otherwise. They frequently act as host escorts for travelers in their area and give short-term lodging.

The Globetrotter's manual, with its frequent updates, as well as their newsletter, gives timely travel updates and ongoing feedback from their lively peripatetic group.

With almost two-thirds of its membership age 35 or under, Globetrotters is oriented toward the younger group, or at least toward the young at heart. The Globetrotter specialty, as often as not, is the kind of travel that you would describe as not run-of-the-mill.

INNter Lodging Co-op Services, Inc.

P.O. Box 7044
Tacoma, WA 98407
Phone: (206) 756-0343

Director:

Robert Ehrenheim

Started:

INNter Lodging was begun in 1980.

Size:

INNter Lodging has a membership of about 300 members.

Subscription Fees: (annually)

Subscriber (family):	$95
Student subscriber:	$10
(with family membership)	

Membership is for the remainder of the current year plus the next. Calendar membership year is May 1 - April 30.

Directories:

The directory is published in August of each year. Listings give professions/occupations, age categories, interests, nearby large towns and local sights to see.

Types of Listings:

INNter Lodging is a lodging cooperative serving as a greater family to provide shelter for members. The host family provides appropriate beds, bedding, linens, towels and either a common or private bath. It is not a bed-and-breakfast program, although in some instances the host may offer foodstuff at an agreed-to fee. The nightly lodging fee is $4 (common bath) or $5 (private bath) per person. Children with sleeping bags pay .50.

Most of the lodging hosts accept children, and a large percentage welcome the handicapped. It is a good idea for the handicapped to clarify details since not all of these homes are equipped to handle wheelchairs. All members agree to make their homes available for at least four months a year, but they accept guests only at their convenience.

Exchanger Profile:

A wide variety of professions make up the membership, with teachers comprising about 25% of the group. Almost a third of the members are retired per the current directory, and most of the subscribers fall into the age 45+ category.

Subscriber Mix:

USA listings account for 90% of the subscribers. The USA listings are strongest in the Pacific West - California, Washington and Oregon - with Colorado also included. Florida, New York, Maryland and Texas are strong states, and 42 of the states are represented altogether.

Foreign listings are limited, found mainly in Canada with a few in England, Holland, Belgium, South Africa, Switzerland and Austria.

Club Strengths and Weaknesses:

INNter Lodging offers bargain cooperative stays in homes that provide double or twin beds and common or private baths. Children may have to bring sleeping bags, and the handicapped are hosted but need to check ahead of time to ensure that accommodations are adequate.

For the independent traveler who wishes a short-term hospitality stay, or several short-term tandem stays, especially on a junket of the Pacific West, the opportunities are excellent. Several of the other states also have a great deal to offer the overnight lodger on the move. Listings for hospitality stays abroad are limited.

The Hospitality Exchange

116 Coleridge
San Francisco, CA 94110
Phone: (415) 826-8248

Directors:

Lee Glickstein and Joy-Lily

Started:

The Hospitality Exchange was started in 1988 as direct successor to the Travelers Directory which ceased publishing in 1986. The Travelers Directory was a 30-year-old network that helped pioneer hospitality exchanging and was one of the largest in the field.

Size:

The membership for 1990 was 285.

Subscription Fees: (annually)

Subscriber: $15

Membership includes the immediate household and is for the calendar year.

Directories:

The Hospitality Exchange publishes 3 directories per year - in March, July and October. Your listing appears in one of the directories unless your vital information changes or the listing contains an error. As a member, you are sent all 3 directories regardless of when you join. Only members listed in the directory may participate in exchanges.

Types of Listings:

Members listed in the directory offer hospitality to other members, which usually means lodging for one or two nights. Anything more than this must be negotiated. Meals are not included but some listings indicate they are offered by the host. Accommodations include beds, floor, couch and tent space. Each listing carries a descriptive paragraph of the facilities and interests of the member or household.

Exchanger Profile:

The occupations and professions of the subscribers run the gamut - teachers, artists, doctors, sales people, students, writers. The current directory shows more than two-thirds of the membership under age 45.

Subscriber Mix:

Per current directories, two-thirds of the subscribers are in the USA. While listings cover 35 of the states, California accounts for the most with New York also strong.

Foreign listings are found in 25 or more countries and are growing. Germany shows the most, with East European countries such as Czechoslovakia, Poland and Yugoslavia also represented. Holland, France, Australia and Canada make the next best showings after Germany.

Club Strengths and Weaknesses:

The Hospitality Exchange has a fast-growing, younger membership worldwide. Its greatest strength is in the USA, notably California. Growing interest abroad, especially in the East European countries, indicates an expected membership increase in those areas.

The World For Free

c/o Seidboard World Enterprises
P.O. Box 137, Prince Street Station
New York, NY 10012
Phone: (212) 674-7018

Director:

Mykel Board

Started:

The World For Free began operation in 1986.

Size:

Membership runs about 150 subscribers.

Subscription Fees: (annually)

Subscriber: $25

Directories:

The club publishes two directories and two updates per year. The main directories are published in January and June, with the two updates coming out in March and September.

The directory listing includes your name, address, phone number and whatever else you want to say about yourself. The subscriber gets a confidential membership number which can be checked via a simple phone call. The directory includes photographs of the members as further identification.

Directories contain useful travel tips on discount airlines, bus travel, economy hostels, how to get a free car for travel, information about the ride-share system in Europe and more.

Types of Listings:

Directory listings include hospitality exchanges or hospitality offered. Lodging is usually for one to three nights, with a maximum of four nights, unless the host offers more. Listings also include members who want to exchange apartments for longer stays.

Exchanger Profile:

Members tend to be younger and more mobile than most hospitality exchangers. The World For Free came about through Mykel Board's contacts in the music business while touring America and Europe with his rock'n'roll band. Many of the members are artists, musicians or music lovers. Entire bands can list themselves together and pay only one membership fee. Members indicate if they can accommodate an entire touring group.

Subscriber Mix:

The World For Free has members in 29 of the USA states. Most of these are in New York and California. Membership is divided almost evenly between the USA and countries abroad.

Listings are found in Australia, Belgium, Canada, Czechoslovakia, Denmark, Finland, Germany, Hungary, Ireland, Japan,Kenya, the Netherlands, Norway, Peru, Poland, Switzerland, Turkey, the United Kingdom and Yugoslavia. Germany shows the most listings abroad, followed by Poland.

Club Strengths and Weaknesses;

The World For Free offers almost an even mix of domestic and foreign subscribers. Opportunities abroad are best in Germany and Poland. The young, very mobile and artistically inclined group of subscribers indicates that the directory listings are used often and that those acting as hosts generally are also travelers.

Subscriber mobility leads to some instability. There is a good chance that any one of the members might suddenly leave town and travel for an extended period and may not be as available as members of the more staid hospitality exchange clubs.

U.S. Servas Committee, Inc.

11 John Street
New York, NY 10038
Phone: (212) 267-0252

Started:

Started in 1948, Servas was founded as a non-profit, cultural traveler/host organization that operates on a volunteer basis to help build goodwill and understanding among the peoples of the world.

Size:

The exact numbers of hosts and travelers throughout the world is hard to estimate, but a rough count would be 6,000 to 8,000 at any given time.

Subscription Fees: (annually)

Traveler fee:	$45
Host contribution:	$15
Host List use:	$15

Directories:

Host directories are published by each member country, some 100 at present. Host lists are requested for the countries or areas where you wish to travel. USA area representatives are listed as contacts in 40 of the states. These host lists give the host's address, phone number, languages spoken, profession, interests and how many people a host can accommodate at one time. Independent contact is made by travelers with the hosts. Travelers must be at least 18 years old, unless accompanied by family.

Types of Listings:

Servas is intended not as a cheap way to travel but for the thoughtful traveler who wants to know individuals by entering their homes as one of the family and sharing experiences, ideas and activities. You share the everyday life of the hosts whom you visit, and the stays are usually for two days unless you are invited for longer. No money changes hands, although travelers invited for meals and other favors usually reciprocate with some gift of their own. U.S. Servas also welcomes travelers with physical disabilities.

Subscriber Mix:

More than 2,000 Servas hosts are located in the USA. The majority of their guests are from other countries, but interchange between USA hosts and domestic travelers is commonplace.

The Servas hosts are found in more than 120 countries around the world. Germany shows more than 1,300 hosts, India and Japan about 400 each, Austria under 100 and Portugal fewer than 50. The remaining countries have lesser numbers of hosts. Hosts in the metropolitan and popular tourist areas get the most requests.

Program Strengths and Weaknesses:

Servas offers an international membership that probably includes more countries than any other hospitality program. Its estimated membership of 6,000 to 8,000 at any given time is one of the largest hospitality stay programs.

The almost evenly divided mix of USA and foreign hosts provides excellent opportunities for both the USA and foreign travelers. Servas offers travel with a purpose in its emphasis on sharing at a personal level, which leads to deeper international understanding and serves as a basis for world peace.

12
Bed-and-Breakfast Exchanges

Bed-and-breakfast as a travel alternative has long been popular in European countries, especially Britain. Within the last decade the bed-and-breakfast movement has rapidly gained momentum in the USA and now, more and more, is becoming a favorite with travelers. While rates for accommodations vary from the economical to the expensive, the price trend has been upward so that the average nightly rate per individual now runs around $50 or more.

The hospitality exchange, with its economical lodging, promises to become the new bed-and-breakfast movement of the 1990s. Within the hospitality exchange club network, certain clubs which offer bed-and-breakfast exchange exclusively have begun to appear on the scene. The following are worth looking into.

Educator's B & B Exchange

Box 5279
Eugene, OR 97405
Phone: 1-800-872-8835

Directors:

Norm and Hazel Smith

Started:

Educator's B & B Exchange began operation in 1987.

Size:

The current directory shows almost 500 listings. The director indicates that membership exceeds 800.

Subscription Fees: (annually)

Membership fee:	$25
Initiation fee:	$10
Room per night:	$22
Booking fee:	$ 6

Directories:

Educator's B & B Exchange publishes one directory per year in April. As new members join, the exchange sends you updates to attach to the directory. The directory gives the member's first name only, his city of location, background, interests and hobbies, as well as a description of the home, amenities and the area. Last name, street address and telephone number of the member are not given in order to preserve privacy.

From the directory you choose your desired accommodations then write or phone the director with your travel dates. The director contacts the members you have chosen and requests accommodations for your specified dates. After confirming your request, the director gives you the host's name, address and phone number. You contact the host directly to work out time of arrival or other details.

The cost of a room per night is $22 for a single member or $22 per night for a member and spouse or companion. Floor space for one child under 12 years of age who travels with you is free. You pay a $6 booking fee for each stay, without regard to the length of stay. Each night a member or a member and his companion stay in your home, you will earn $8 in Travel Credits. You can use this credit to help pay for your lodging expense at another member's home, or it will be applied to your annual membership fee.

Types of Listings:

Members of the network provide a spare room in their homes for other members. In exchange, they have the opportunity to stay in the home of any other member. A clean, comfortable place to sleep is provided, and a serve-yourself continental breakfast is included.

Exchanger Profile:

Educator's B & B Exchange is open to all educators (former and retired), the support staff of educators, and the immediate family of both. The director indicates that a growing segment of the membership is retired, probably 30% currently and increasing.

Subscriber Mix:

Educator's B & B Exchange listings in the current directory show more than 450 entries for the USA. California is especially strong with over 100 listings, as is New York with 60 or so. Other states that indicate membership strength are Massachusetts, Michigan, Washington, Ohio, Oregon, Connecticut, Florida and Maine. Forty-five of the states are represented, including Hawaii and Alaska.

Club Strengths and Weaknesses:

Educator's B & B Exchange is a fast-growing network of travel-minded educators whose goal is to reduce the cost of traveling. Besides being easy on your pocketbook, the bed-and-breakfast network brings educators together to share experiences, making their travel more meaningful. Members like the opportunity to meet hosts and guests with similar backgrounds and interests.

Foreign listings are limited at present.

TIE Bed and Breakfast Exchange

356 Boylston Street
Boston, MA 02116
Phone: (617) 536-5651

Director:

Jan Stankus

Started:

The TIE (Traveler's Information Exchange) Bed and Breakfast Exchange program was established in 1986.

(Traveler's Information Exchange, known until 1977 as Women's Rest Tour Association, was founded 1891 by Julia Ward Howe. TIE is one of the country's oldest travel clubs and was originally an all-female organization founded expressly to furnish its members with the information needed to take vacations. At a time when women were not expected to travel alone, some gutsy women set up the networking organization to tell each other what they needed to know. The information and recommendations about travel and lodging was pretty basic stuff. This service is still offered by the club to its now mixed clientele of male and female.)

Size:

From a peak of 6,000 members in the 1920s, TIE club membership has dropped to a current total of about 500, as new information sources have become available to travelers.

To keep pace with the times and the needs of its membership, TIE now includes the bed-and-breakfast option for its travelers. The Bed and Breakfast Exchange program lists just over 50 TIE members who currently participate.

Subscription Fees: (annually)

First-year TIE membership:	$25
Dues for subsequent years:	$15

Directories:

The Bed and Breakfast List, which is available to TIE members only, gives the name, address and phone number of participating members. The membership is stable, showing few changes since the first directory published for 1986-87. All members receive a helpful newsletter, The Traveler.

Types of Listings:

Bed-and-breakfast listings only are included in the directory. The hospitality gesture is intended as a benefit of TIE membership rather than as a money-making venture. A small donation (currently $9 per night per person) is paid by the guest to compensate the host for food and linens.

Exchanger Profile:

TIE Bed and Breakfast Exchange shows a solid, stable base of experienced travelers.

Subscriber Mix:

USA listings in the current directory include 20 states, with Massachusetts accounting for a fourth of the listings. Most of the other listings are found in Connecticut, New Jersey, Michigan, Pennsylvania, North Carolina, Maine, New Hampshire, Ohio, Virginia and Florida.

Foreign listings are minimal, with only the two countries of Mexico and Uruguay included.

Club Strengths and Weaknesses:

Traveler's Information Exchange is comprised of a largely upscale, professional membership. Once practically unknown outside Boston Brahmin circles, TIE has begun to raise its profile with added services such as the Bed and Breakfast Exchange. The main drawback of the Bed and Breakfast Exchange at present is the limited membership which is confined primarily to the New England area.

13
Homestays

Another alternative to traditional travel is the homestay, which is a variation upon the hospitality exchange that usually consists of travel with primarily a meaningful purpose.

Homestays are generally sponsor-arranged, usually non-profit, and involve a stay of longer duration than the typical hospitality exchange. As a rule, the stated purpose behind such hospitality stays is to encourage understanding and culture-sharing among people of different countries and/or promote world peace.

Most often, the homestay is not a reciprocal exchange. It is a visit with an established host that typically covers two or three weeks but may run for a month or more. Ordinarily, little or no money changes hands except for a small administrative fee. Club membership is seldom required, and directories of membership listings are not often used.

To arrange a homestay, you will need to sign up with a sponsor, indicate your interests and await placement, or acceptance, if such is required. Sponsors handle the details of matchmaking.

Afterwards, you may be given the name and address of your host so you can correspond prior to the visit. Some sponsors help arrange travel, or even act as hosts on the travel itinerary.

Different from the exchange that is tied to study, teaching or work, the goodwill homestay is travel-oriented, but travel with a meaningful gesture. If you prefer this type of travel or just wish to act as a host for such travelers, you can acquaint yourself with some of what is available through the following groups.

American Host

P.O. Box 803
Garden Grove, CA 92642
Phone: (714) 537-5711
FAX: (714) 537-5798

Director:

Wayne A. Clark

Started:

American Host was started in 1962

Size:

Since inception of the American Host program, more than 40,000 American families have opened their homes to 15,000 English-speaking teachers, librarians and school administrators in Western Europe, with Australia and New Zealand now included. In a typical year, American Host families receive about 200 visiting educators from Western Europe.

Matchmaking Procedure:

Directories are not used but instead educators are informed about the program through professional associations in their own countries. Those interested educators fill out an application specifying the area in the USA they would like to visit. Matching of host families and their guests is based on compatible interests determined from host home questionnaires and applicant interviews. Those matched are given each other's addresses and names in order that they may get acquainted by correspondence before they meet in America.

Types of Listings:

American Host is a non-profit program designed to show the American way of life to overseas educators through pairing them with American families. Almost anyone can qualify as a host family to entertain a guest or guests for one or two weeks. Host families need not be educators. You simply fill out a host home application indicating your preference for the number of guests and length of stay. All participating visitors are required to speak English.

As a host, you meet the guests upon arrival and offer hospitality including a private room and meals for up to two weeks. Between July 1 and August 1, European participants fly to the USA and spend four weeks in the chosen geographical area with two or three host families. American Host contracts with a travel agency on the basis of lowest possible price for domestic and international travel for the guests. There is an additional administrative fee which amounts to about 20% of the air fare.

If you are a California resident, you may opt for the "Down Under" program. Visiting educators from Australia and New Zealand arrive during the winter season, their "summer break," starting about January 3. They spend 11 days with a host family in either northern or southern California and then travel to the opposite region for an additional 11-day stay with another host family.

Participant Profile:

All participating visitors are teachers, librarians or administrators. Visitors are all English-speaking and have traditionally come from Western Europe. Guests have participated from such countries as Austria, Belgium, Finland, France, Germany, Holland, Italy, Switzerland and the United Kingdom. The Australia and New Zealand guest program began in 1990. Host families need not be educators. All host families are in the USA, and all participating visitors come from Western Europe, Australia or New Zealand.

Program Strengths and Weaknesses:

The American Host program gives you and your family an opportunity to enjoy meaningful and rewarding travel or hosting experiences while promoting friendship and better understanding. While visitor participation is restricted to educators, hosting is not. The program is limited to the summer months of July and August for European visitors and the winter month of January for Australian and New Zealander guests. Although the American Host program is not designed as a reciprocal exchange, many host families do make later return visits to the homes of their guests. In fact, this has become an exciting part of the program according to feedback received.

Friends In France

P.O. Box 1044
Rocky Hill, CT 06067
Phone: (203) 563-0195

Director:

Cher Powell and Henry Stark

Started:

Friends in France was originally started in the 1970s. The current program began its operation in 1988.

Size:

The current directory includes 42 chateaus, manor houses, farmhouses and country houses in France that participate in the homestay program.

In addition, 21 furnished unoccupied apartments are listed for rent in central Paris.

Subscription Fees:

Booking for each homestay: $20
No membership is required.

Homestay costs start at $30 per day per person including a French breakfast. Costs may range to $65 per day per person, with meals extra (dinner $9 to $25).

Directories:

Friends in France puts out a yearly directory available for $7 describing the homestay families, their homes and regions, with photos and illustrations.

Interested visitors fill out a brief questionnaire indicating their regions or homes of choice, dates and length of stay planned, and other preferences. Payment in full is made once reservations have been confirmed.

Types of Listings:

Friends in France does not accept hosts who are interested merely in renting out a room or in a bed-and-breakfast operation. Only those hosts who have a genuine desire to know their guests and offer them hospitality are enlisted. All facilities are visited on an average of once a year and most have a wonderful track record according to the directors.

The homestays offer a variety of flexibility. Meals are optional, as is the amount of time spent with the host family. Hosted tours and driving services are often available. Linens and fresh towels are provided, but you will be expected to straighten your own quarters and take care of laundry. Children are welcome and if you wish to practice your French, host families will refrain from speaking English.

The host homes do not want to be used as bed-and-breakfast stops by transients nor as boarding houses by permanent guests. As a result a minimum stay of 3 nights and a maximum stay of two weeks in any one family is imposed. Many clients choose to visit more than one family, and some guests have visited as many as eight families on a trip. Whatever you wish, the club will be happy to work with you.

In addition to the host homes, Friends in France offers a variety of furnished apartments for rent in central Paris.

Listings Profile:

Owners of lovely manor houses, chateaus and farm-houses with centuries-old family history make up the listings. They are located in all areas of France. Each home, with its family background and surrounding attractions, is described in the directory.

Program Strengths and Weaknesses:

The main attraction of Friends in France is that it offers a flexible vacation and cultural experience with delightful French families who are eager to share their lives with their guests. While the hospitality is not free, the costs are generally cheaper than local hotels, and you get much more for your money than the usual paying guest.

Mobility International USA

P.O. Box 3551
Eugene, OR 97403
Phone: (503) 343-1284 (Voice & TDD)

Size:

Mobility International USA has over 500 members.

Subscription Fees: (annually)

Full membership: $20
Quarterly newsletter only: $10

Types of Listings:

Mobility International USA is a national non-profit organization whose purpose is to promote and facilitate international exchange and recreational travel experiences for people with disabilities. MIUSA is committed to the goal of integrating people with disabilities into existing avenues of leisure travel and international exchange.

Full membership entitles you to use of their information and referral services, discounts on international exchange programs sponsored by MIUSA, and the quarterly newsletter, Over the Rainbow.

MIUSA offers sponsored host family homestay programs which allow you to share your home with a disabled international exchange participant from another country or to stay abroad with a host family.

One of their publications, A Guide to International Educational Exchange, Community Service, and Travel for Persons with Disabilities, covers 75 international educational exchange programs and community service projects with information on how persons who are blind, deaf, or have mobility limitations can participate. It includes information about homestay opportunities.

These are the affiliate members of Mobility International worldwide:

Denmark: Claus Loeschenkohl
Mellemfolkeligt Samvirke
Borgergade 12 - 14
DK-1300 Copenhagen K
Denmark

England: Mobility International
International Headquarters
228 Borough High Street
London SE1 1JX
England

France: Veronique Claude
CNFLRH
38 Blvd. Raspail
F-75007 Paris
France

Germany: Annerose Hintzke
Mobility International Germany
c/o BAG-C
Eupenerstrasse 5
D-6500 Mainz
Federal Republic of Germany

W. Africa: Thomas Abukari
Mobility International Ghana
c/o P.O. Box 535
Tamale, Ghana
West Africa

India: Pradip Mallick
        Nat'l Fed. of Orthopedically Handicapped
        BT Road (Bonhooghly)
        Calcutta 700 090
        India

Ireland: Colm O'Doherty
          Irish Wheelchair Association
          Aras Chuchulain
          Blackheath Drive
          Clontarf, Dublin 3
          Ireland

Italy: Franca Tavazzani
        Associasione Per L'Assistenza
        Via San Barnaba 29
        I-20122 Milano
        Italy

Malta: John Micallef
        Physically Handicapped Rehab. Fund
        Rehabilitation Centre
        Malta

Netherlands: Henk Willemsen
        Mobility International Netherlands
        Postbus 165
        NL-6560 AD Groesbeek
        Netherlands

N. Ireland: Brian Symington
Mobility International N. Ireland
c/o Eastern Health & Social Services Board
12-22 Linenhall Street
Belfast BIf2 1BS
Northern Ireland

Switzerland: Mobility International Switzerland
Postfach 129
Feldeggstrasse 71
CH-8032 Zurich
Switzerland

People To People Gifu

c/o The Juroku Bank, Ltd.
Two World Financial Center, 36th Floor
New York, NY 10281
Phone: (212) 786-1620

Director:

Hirohiko Kouchi

Started:

People to People Gifu was begun in 1981

Size:

About 100 foreign exchanges are arranged each year.

Subscription Fees:

Administrative fee: 5,000 yen per person.

Matchmaking Procedure:

You submit an application indicating date and length of stay, number in party, and other information. The Gifu contact handles placement in a home or homes.

Types of Listings:

All homestays are in the Gifu Prefecture, located in the center of the Japanese archipelago.   The length of a homestay is seven days maximum in one host family, but you may spend more than a month in one area if you wish. The host family provides meals and bed and bath free of charge and takes time to entertain the guests.

Participant Profile:

Participants come from various countries but mainly from the USA, and all participants are from outside Japan. All professions/occupations and age groups are represented, singles and families, with the ages of participants varying from from age 8 to age 72.

Program Strengths and Weaknesses:

People to People Gifu provides a bridge of friendship and goodwill between Gifu and foreign countries. It offers an exciting and unique chance for foreign visitors to share the warmth of personal interest and respect that leads to many lasting friendships. The half dozen provinces of Gifu contain a wealth of cultural and scenic attraction for the visitor. The program is limited to about 100 homestays yearly and all homestays are in the area of Gifu Prefecture.

Seniors Abroad International Homestay

12533 Pacato Circle North
San Diego, CA 92128
Phone: (619) 485-1696

Director:

Evelyn Zivetz

Started:

The Seniors Abroad homestay program was started in 1984

Size:

Since 1984 more than 1,500 hosts and guests have taken part in the international homestay, a non-profit program.

Matchmaking Procedure:

You sign up for the tour of your choice, and upon receiving your application the director matches the guests with hosts. When a match is arranged, names and addresses are sent to each host and guest so that they may correspond prior to the homestay. The director also arranges the international travel as well as the in-country travel.

Types of Listings:

Participants are limited to single persons or couples over-50 who want opportunities for personal international experiences. Each program includes a maximum of 20 travelers. You may take part in the program as either a host or a traveler or both.

In all programs, guests are welcomed as members of the host family, with hospitality voluntary on the part of the host and without cost to the guest. Costs include the international flight, orientation in-country, and bed-and-breakfast or hotel-and-breakfast while en route. A typical homestay tour lasts three weeks and currently runs upwards of $2,000.

Participant Profile:

All participants are age 50-plus. Evelyn Zivetz founded Seniors Abroad after living in Japan for three years when her husband was based at the American Embassy in Tokyo. At first, the homestays were limited to Japanese and American travelers, but in 1986 Seniors Abroad was expanded to include the Scandinavian countries of Denmark, Sweden and Norway. In 1989 the program was further expanded to include Australia and New Zealand.

Program Strengths and Weaknesses:

Seniors Abroad is a non-profit program that provides international homestay experiences for the over-50 traveler. It offers the best of both the individual hospitality homestay and the semi-conducted tour for those who like to leave some of the arrangements to others. Homestays with three or four different hosts on an itinerary provide variety and a broad basis for learning how others live in a foreign culture. Many hosts and guests continue to write each other over the years. Since there is no charge for the actual homestay, the cost of the program is not prohibitive.

In that Seniors Abroad has the cooperation of the American Embassy-USIS, the travel group gets a courtesy orientation at the American Embassy of each respective country. Another plus of the program is that all homestays may be extended.

Currently the program is limited to arranged homestays between Americans and travelers from Japan, the Scandinavian countries, Australia and New Zealand. You may choose whether you wish to participate as a guest traveler or as a host or as both.

A certain amount of flexibility is required for the traveler who wishes to become a part of the program. Usually the Australia/New Zealand stays begin in February, the Scandinavian stays in August/September, and the Japan trips in October. For those hosting travelers in the USA, the Scandinavian guests come in April, those from Japan in May, and the Australia/New Zealand guests in June/July.

The Experiment In International Living

P.O. Box 595
Putney, VT 05346
Phone: (802) 387-4210
Telex: (650) 349-0251 MCI UW
FAX: (802) 387-5783

Started:

Experiment in International Living, the oldest educational and cultural exchange organization, was started in 1932. The individual homestay program for adults is one of its many programs.

Size:

Experiment In International Living is a worldwide federation with 27 organizations. Each has its own network of local representatives who recruit and orient host families within their community. The individual homestay program is currently offered in 19 countries, and just under 1,000 people per year take advantage of this program worldwide.

Subscription Fees:

A program fee of $100 to $400 covers the administrative costs. In some countries, the local representatives and host families are paid a small stipend to cover their extra expenses.

Matchmaking Procedure:

You request an application for the individual homestay program for the country of interest. The application indicates your desired length of homestay (1 to 4 weeks limit), preferred start date, your interests and objectives. Once accepted, you will be notified of the host family name and address so you can make final transportation arrangements to their town.

Types of Listings:

The program consists of individual homestays of 1 to 4 weeks for adults. The program is non-profit and emphasizes personal involvement in the life of another culture. The homestay is regarded as a learning experience. Sharing the daily routine, customs and language with another family broadens one's horizons and often leads to lifelong friendships.

Participant Profile:

Application for the homestay program is open to all adults. Requirements vary according to country, but this usually means 18 years and up. While the length of stay may run from 1 to 4 weeks, the average stay is two weeks.

Of the almost 1,000 participants each year, about one-third are visitors from overseas who come to the USA for homestays. A smaller group of about 10% of the total are USA citizens visiting other countries. The remaining participants, some 60%, are individuals from foreign countries visiting foreign countries; i.e., the USA is not involved.

Program Strengths and Weaknesses:

The Experiment in International Living is the oldest educational and cultural exchange program. The homestay program provides excellent opportunity for travel with a purpose in 19 countries abroad. The program is well-suited to the independent traveler who wants to travel with a purpose yet not be bound by an itinerary imposed by a group or organization. You pick the country you want to visit, and you pick the dates.

14
Profile Of A "Hospitality" Trip

(Reprint of an article by the author entitled, "Take Your Own Oregon Trail Hospitality Style.")

If you like vacation travel without the usual huge outlay for lodging and if you enjoy sightseeing that extends to real-life living at the local level, try hospitality stays, the bed-and-breakfast movement of the 1990s.

My wife and I did just that on a one-week tour of the Pacific Northwest this summer. On a round of hospitality stays, we found all those things that travelers hope for — new friends, real hospitality, virtually free lodging, and the excitement of adventurous travel.

Our first night out we stayed in Sacramento with Lee Ann in a rambling house set back on wooded grounds. Her husband built the house, she told us at the kitchen table where we talked until late. It was the first Tudor-style in the neighborhood. Since Lee Ann was sleeping in next morning, we let ourselves out, leaving a note saying, "Thank you. On to Oregon." Alongside the note, we left $10, our total lodging fee for the night. No check-out, no bell boys, tips nor tax. Just a couple of bags thrown into the car, and we were off up Interstate 5 through the center of northern California.

Our real Oregon Trail had begun at our home in Fresno, California, only a few days earlier when we scanned hospitality club directories for members along our projected itinerary. With homes identified, we made a few simple calls to arrange lodging and were off on our round of Lewis and Clark adventure, 1990 style.

A hospitality exchange is nothing more than a net-work of friendly, travel-oriented people who provide hospitality to strangers in their homes. You offer a spare room or bed to travelers for a short stay when they come to your city. In exchange, they or other members of the network will usually do the same for you when you visit their town. As a rule, little or no exchange of money is involved. The $10 we left for Lee Ann is the nightly lodging fee (for two) required of INNter Lodging Club members.

The easiest way to exchange hospitality is to join one of the clubs and get your name into its directory of listings. Or, better still, join several of the clubs. This will give you access to thousands of listings worldwide. You can choose from any number of clubs, and the fees are unbelievably low, usually well under $50 per year. From there on, next to nothing is required in the way of plan-ning. Just write or telephone ahead to members living where you want to stay and arrange for the desired number of nights if available.

Although we had scheduled our second night for Medford, Oregon, we arrived early and decided to push on to nearer Portland. Tom, a retired photographer, and Rosemary, a nurse, gave us a rain check for next time through. This schedule change called for a motel stay in Eugene, where we spent this off-night in a tobacco-cured, $45 room, another way to go if you feel more comfortable paying.

When next day we arrived at St. Helens, a half hour north of Portland where the Columbia River begins its final 50-mile run to the Pacific out at Astoria, Esther, our hospitality hostess, pronounced, "You will need more than one day to see Portland." We agreed on three nights and she showed us to our upstairs quarters - three bedrooms, a bath, sitting room, and an already open window by our bed.

"Houston, Portland, Milwaukee, St. Helens, computers, the airlines," Esther reeled off where her six sons and one daughter now live and the work they do. She has made a quilt for each of the 29 grandchildren. The pink one there still on the shelf — she had anticipated too freely. The last two grandchildren had been boys.

Portland hits you with a kaleidoscope of things you want to see and do all at once. With Esther's help, we spent the next two days unravelling Portland: Converging rivers, breezy, arching bridges with their green-steel trademark superstructures. Washington Park and its enormous rose garden, with plaques embedded in the walkways announcing the names of rose queens since 1907. Jake's Seafood (specializing in crawfish), since 1892. Old Country Buffet (a lucky find at 82nd and Causey) with patrons lined up out the door. Across the Columbia River to Washington state slashed prices at the Pendleton Mills outlet, in Washougal.

Esther directed us to the Bridge of the Gods at Cascade Locks where a stern-wheeler riverboat captain guided us to that very spot where the natural land bridge (the original Bridge of the Gods) once spanned the Columbia River. Huge boulders, fragments of the collapsed archway (the captain said) disported themselves right there in the river to prove its once-upon-a-time existence.

Along the banks, Indians on jerry-rigged, cantilevered platforms exercised their year-round treaty fishing rights, one fisherman struggling up an embankment with his catch-of-the-day, using both hands. Coho Charlie, the captain told us, his platform just to the left there, has a better approach to fishing. He fills a washtub with fertilized salmon eggs, lets them hatch, then dumps them into the river. Everybody knows that salmon return to their birthplace for spawning. Next year, these same salmon swim back upriver and "jump into Charlie's tub." We were in tall tale country, Paul Bunyan territory. We looked for Bigfoot, or his alias Sasquatch, along the banks.

Esther awaited us afterwards with her famous, complimentary marathon car tour of St. Helens. Down through the old town where the courthouse fronted on the river. Two-decker houseboats, rimmed with flower boxes, tied up at the dock. A huge flagpole and flag at the edge of the river. Lots of local gossip. Irby, who owns the houseboat company and is running for the state legislature, donated the flagpole. Most people think it blocks the river view. That is his houseboat with the helicopter on top. Little things you don't learn through a tour bus window.

With the hospitality stay, members frequently offer their guests added amenities. These may include tours, extended stays, meals or other hospitality gestures.

These should not be expected unless spelled out ahead of time, but do not be surprised if they are offered, or you may negotiate for them.

Paying our lodging fee of $30 to Esther, we crossed the Columbia for our third and last hospitality stay, with Bill and Barbara, at Kelso, just inside Washington on the Cowlitz River. This is the river that all the ash and mud and trees had come down when Mt. St. Helens exploded in 1980, they told us. You still find infiltrated ash under the carpet if you look.

Next day, which happened to be the Fourth of July, Bill and Barbara were to take us to Mt. St. Helens for a look at its tangled, toothpick forest of giant fir felled by the thermoclastic blast. And that night we celebrated the Fourth, with several thousand others, around a lake in the central park at Longview — live band, beer sausage, fireworks, a light rain, a sea of blanket-covered heads.

With our round of hospitality stays ended, for now, we "settled up" with our hosts and took leave. Our total cost for the two nights' lodging, amenities and all, was "no charge." An hour's sprint west along the Columbia River, in the tracks of Lewis and Clark, got us to its mouth, where a modern, steel bridge now spans the river's expanse seeing Highway 101 safely to the Washington side, the terminus on this day all but hidden in fog.

"We call it the bridge to nowhere," the service station attendant told us.

Having seen the Oregon Trail to its end, we headed home down Highway 101.

The morning saw us drive down a breath-taking coast to Seaport, with its creamy salt-water taffy, rattlesnake beer and real Oregon blackberry wine for tourist take-home presents. Then Tillamook and cheddar cheese. The afternoon found us in Newport and Mo's cafe—slumgullion (chowder filled with shrimp), salad heaped with more shrimp, thick toasted garlic-butter bread, $13 for two. We treated ourselves to a beach front stay at Shiloh Inn in Newport for $70, because there were no homestay candidates in the area.

The following whirlwind day brought us through more see-it-to-believe-it Oregon coastal landscapes past such places as Yachats and Bandon, with captain plate dining overlooking the dock where working boats unloaded their salmon, chinook and coho, with an incidental ling cod or red snapper that slipped in.

The coast was dazzling, but this last lap of the trip was different. We were again merely sightseers, tourists, outsiders. We never quite got beneath the surface of things the way we had when visiting with Lee Ann and Esther and Bill and Barbara. Maybe another day, when we have more time and the hospitality exchange clubs have more coastal lodging to offer, we will do up that stretch of the trip again and see its other, hidden dimension.

"Don't hospitality exchangers run into surprises?'" the apprehensive sometimes ask.

"A great many," we answer. "Mostly good ones."

Hospitality exchanging is not for everyone, but it is tailor-made for the person who prefers independent travel. If you are the creative type who likes to plan his or her own vacation, make all the important decisions, choose what you will do and when—without being locked into a tour schedule—then the vacation hospitality exchange is probably for you. Those who need the security of conventional, full-service, travel-agent touring should not apply.

Aside from independence, hospitality exchanging offers the most for those flexible and inquisitive travelers who enjoy meeting people and making new friends. And if you are one of the fortunate few who travel with a sense of adventure and imagination, looking for possibilities in the turns of your itinerary, you are especially well-suited to hospitality exchanging. If this describes you, go ahead and try the hospitality exchange. You are almost sure to like it.

As with any adventure, there is always risk. But aside from the occasional exception, hospitality exchangers are dependable people just like yourself. They are usualy professional people who have the same interests and concerns and appreciate the same courtesies.

Back in Fresno, we figured up our total lodging outlay for the trip, which included a final night's motel stay in northern. It amounted to $207.

We had just experienced a travel adventure that few tourists ever do, and we had done it at less than bankruptcy prices.

Is this any way to travel? We think it is.

Appendix A
USA State and Territorial
Tourist Offices

Free informational vacation materials are available upon request from the following USA state and territorial tourist offices. A letter or call, often to a toll-free 800 number, will bring their great variety of useful publications to either your exchange partners or yourself.

These tourist offices will gladly supply you with such items as maps, calendars of events, travel guides and brochures for the areas which you wish to visit. The materials usually contain information about accommodations, campgrounds, restaurants, attractions and recreational activities as well.

Your request should indicate any specific materials you want in addition to the general packet — information about fishing, camping, bed-and-breakfast, skiing. Ask if the office also has special publications which are not routinely sent unless you request them.

Alabama Bureau of Tourism and Travel
532 South Perry Street, Dept. TIA
Montgomery, AL 36104-4614
Phone: (205) 261-4169
Toll Free:
In-State: 1-800-392-8096
Out-of-State: 1-800-ALABAMA
(Continental USA)

Alaska Division of Tourism
P.O. Box E, TIA
Juneau, AK 99811
Phone: (907) 465-2010

Arizona Office of Tourism
1100 West Washington Avenue, 1100-A
Phoenix, AZ 85007
Phone: (602) 255-4764
Arkansas Tourism Office
One Capitol Mall, Dept. 7701
Little Rock, AR 72201
Phone: (501) 682-7777
Toll Free:
In-State: 1-800-482-8999
Out-of-State: 1-800-643-8383
(Continental USA)

California Office of Tourism
1121 L Street, Suite 103, Dept. TIA
Sacramento, CA 95814
Phone: (916) 322-2881
Toll Free:
1-800-TO CALIF
(Continental USA)

Colorado Tourism Board
1625 Broadway, Suite 1700, COLO #1

Denver, CO 80202
Phone: (303) 592-5410
Toll Free:
  1-800-433-2656
  (Continental USA)

Connecticut Dept. of Economic Development
  Tourism Division
  210 Washington Street, Room 900
  Hartford, CT 06106
  Phone: (203) 566-3948
  Toll Free:
    In-State: 1-800-842-7492
    Out-of-State: 1-800-243-1685
    (Maine to Virginia)

Delaware Tourism Office
  99 Kings Highway, Box 1401, Dept. TIA
  Dover, DE 19903
  Phone: (302) 736-4271
  Toll Free:
    In-State: 1-800-282-8667
    Out-of-State: 1-800-441-8846
    (Continental USA)

Florida Division of Tourism
  126 Van Buren Street, FLDA
  Tallahassee, FL 32399-2000
  Phone: (904) 487-1462

Georgia Dept. of Industry & Trade
  Tourist Division, Dept. TIA
  P.O. Box 1776
  Atlanta, GA 30301
  Phone: (404) 656-3590

Hawaii Visitors Bureau
  P.O. Box 8527, HVB

Honolulu, HI 96815
Phone: (808) 923-1811

Idaho Travel Council
Statehouse Mall, Dept. C
Boise, ID 83720
Phone: (208) 334-2470
Toll Free:
    Out-of-State: 1-800-635-7820
    (Continental USA)

Illinois Tourist Information Center
310 South Michigan, Dept. IOT, Suite 108
Chicago, IL 60604
Phone: (312) 793-2094
Toll Free:
    1-800-223-0121
    (Continental USA)

Indiana Department of Commerce
Tourism Development Division
One North Capitol, Suite 700, IN-DA
Indianapolis, IN 46204
Phone: (317) 232-8860
Toll Free:
    1-800-2-WANDER
    (Continental USA)

Iowa Department of Economic Development
Bureau of Tourism and Visitors
200 East Grand, P.O. Box 6127, TIA
Des Moines, IA 50309
Phone: (515) 281-3100
Toll Free:
    1-800-345-IOWA
    (Continental USA)

Kansas Travel & Tourism Division
400 West 8th, Dept. DIS, 5th Floor
Topeka, KS 66603
Phone: (914) 296-2009

Kentucky Department of Travel Development
2200 Capitol Plaza Tower, Dept. DA
Frankfort, KY 40601
Phone: (502) 564-4930
Toll Free:
1-800-225-TRIP
(USA & Parts of Canada)

Louisiana Office of Tourism
Attention: Inquiry Dept., P.O. Box 94291, LOT
Baton Rouge, LA 70804-9291
Phone: (504) 925-3860
Toll Free:
Out-of-State: 1-800-334-8626
(Continental USA)

Maine Division of Tourism
Maine Publicity Bureau
97 Winthrop Street, Dept. DA
Holwell, ME 04347-2300
Phone: (207) 289-2423
Toll Free:
1-800-533-9595
(Sept.-April: East Coast USA)

Maryland Office of Tourist Development
45 Calvert Street, Dept. A
Annapolis, MD 21401
Phone: (301) 974-3519
Toll Free:
1-800-331-1750, Operator 250
(Continental USA)

Massachusetts Office of Travel & Tourism
100 Cambridge Street, 13th Floor
Boston, MA 02202
Phone: (617) 727-3201 or 3202
Toll Free:
1-800-942-MASS ext. TIA
1-800-624-MASS ext. TIA
(Continental USA)
New England States only
(for summer calendar of events):
1-800-343-9072 ext. TIA

Michigan Travel Bureau
Dept. TIA, P.O. Box 30226
Lansing, MI 48909
Phone: (517) 373-0670
Toll Free:
1-800-5432-YES
(Continental USA)

Minnesota Office of Tourism
375 Jackson Street, Dept. 21
250 Skyway Level
St. Paul, MN 55101
Phone: (612) 296-5029
Toll Free:
In-State: 1-800-652-9747
Out-of-State: 1-800-328-1461
(Continental USA)

Mississippi Division of Tourism
P.O. Box 22825, Dept. T
Jackson, MS 39205
Phone: (601) 359-3426
Toll Free:
1-800-647-2290
(Continental USA)

Missouri Division of Tourism
P.O. Box 1055, Dept. TIA
Jefferson City, MO 65102
Phone (314) 751-4133

Travel Montana
Room 835
Deerlodge, MT 59722
Phone: (406) 444-2654
Toll Free;
Out-of-State: 1-800-541-1447
(Continental USA)

Nebraska Division of Travel & Tourism
P.O. Box 94666, Room 88937
Lincoln, NE 68509-4666
Phone: (402) 471-3794
Toll Free:
In-States: 1-800-742-7595
Out-of-State: 1-800-228-4307
(Continental USA)

Nevada Commission on Tourism
State Capitol Complex, Dept. TIA
Carson City, NV 89710
Phone: (702) 885-3636
Toll Free:
Out-of-State: 1-800-NEVADA 8
(USA and Canada)

New Hampshire Office of Vacation Travel
105 Loudon Road, P.O. Box 856 DA
Concord, NH 03301
Phone: (603) 271-2665

New Jersey Division of Travel & Tourism
20 West State Street, CN 826, Dept. TIA
Trenton, NJ 08625

Phone: (609) 292-2470
Toll Free:
1-800-JERSEY-7

New Mexico Tourism & Travel Division
Joseph M. Montoya Building
1100 St. Francis Drive, Room 777
Santa Fe, MN 87503
Phone: (505) 827-0291
Toll Free:
1-800-545-2040
(Continental USA)

New York State Commerce Department
Operator 3
One Commerce Plaza
Albany, NY 12245
Phone: (518) 474-4116
Toll Free:
1-800-CALL-NYS
(Continental USA)

North Carolina Travel & Tourism Division
430 N. Salisbury, Dept. 867
Raleigh, NC 27611
Phone: (919) 733-4171
Toll Free:
1-800-VISIT NC
(Continental USA)

North Dakota Tourism Promotion
Room 250, Liberty Memorial Building
Capitol Grounds
Bismarck, ND 58505
Phone: (701) 224-2525
Toll Free:
In-State: 1-800-472-2100
Out-of-State: 1-800-437-2077

(Continental USA)
In Canada: 1-800-537-8879

Ohio Division of Travel and Tourism
P.O. Box 1001, Dept. TIA
Columbus, OH 43266-0101
Phone: (614) 466-8844
Toll Free:
1-800-BUCKEYE
(Continental USA)

Oklahoma Tourism & Recreation
Marketing Services Division
500 Will Rogers Building, DA88
Oklahoma City, OK 73105
Phone: (405) 521-2406
Toll Free:
1-800-652-6552

Oregon Economic Development Department
Tourism Division
595 Cottage Street, N.E., Dept. TIA
Salem, OR 97310
Phone: (503) 378-3451
Toll Free:
In-State: 1-800-233-3306
Out-of-State: 1-800-547-7842
(Continental USA)

Pennsylvania Bureau of Travel Development
416 Forum Building, Dept. PR 901
Harrisburg, PA 17120
Phone: (717) 787-5453
Toll Free:
1-800-VISIT PA, ext. 275
(Continental USA)

Rhode Island Department of Economic Development
   Tourism & Promotion
   7 Jackson Walkway, Dept. TIA
   Providence, RI 02903
   Phone: (401) 277-2601
   Toll Free:
   1-800-556-2484
   (ME to VA & Northern Ohio)

South Carolina Division of Tourism
   Box 71, Room 902
   Columbia, SC 29202
   Phone: (803-734-0122

South Dakota Department of Tourism
   Room TIA, Capitol Lake Plaza
   711 Wells Avenue
   Pierre, SD 57501
   Phone: (605) 773-3301
   Toll Free:
       In-State: 1-800-952-3625 or 2217
       Out-of-State: 1-800-843-8000
       (Continental USA)

Tennessee Department of Tourism Development
   P.O. Box 23170, TNDA
   Nashville, TN 37202
   Phone: (615) 741-2158

Texas Tourist Development Agency
   P.O. Box 12008, Dept. TIA
   Austin, TX 78711
   Phone: (512) 462-9191

Utah Travel Council
   Division of Travel Development
   Council Hall/Capitol Hill, Dept. TIA

Salt Lake City, UT 84114
Phone: (801)533-5681

Vermont Travel Division
134 State Street, Dept. TIA
Montpelier, VT 05602
Phone: (802) 828-3236

Virginia Division of Tourism
202 North 9th Street, Suite 500
Dept. VT
Richmond, VA 23219
Phone: (804) 786-2951
Toll Free:
    1-800-VISIT-VA
    (Continental USA)

Washington State Tourism
Development Division
101 General Administration Building
MS AX-13, WASH
Olympia, WA 98504-0613
Phone: (206) 753-5600
Toll Free:
    1-800-544-1800
    (Continental USA)

West Virginia Department of Commerce
Marketing/Tourism Division
2101 Washington Street, E, Dept. TIA
Charleston, WV 25305
Phone: (304) 348-2286
Toll Free:
    1-800-CALL WVA
    (Continental USA)

Wisconsin Division of Tourism Development
    P.O. Box 7606
    Madison, WI 53707
    Phone: (608) 266-2161
    Toll Free:
        1-800-432-TRIP
        (Except NE, HI & AK)

Wyoming Travel Commission
    I-25 and College Drive, Dept. WY
    Cheyenne, WY 82002-0660
    Phone: (307) 777-7777
    Toll Free:
        Out-of-State: 1-800-225-5996

DISTRICT OF COLUMBIA

Washington, DC Convention & Visitors Association
    1575 I Street, N.W., 88STD
    Washington, DC 20005
    Phone: (202) 789-7000

USA TERRITORIES

American Samoa Government
    Office of Tourism
    P.O. Box 1147
    Pago Pago, AS 96799
    Phone: (684) 633-5187 or 5188

Guam Visitors Bureau
    1200 Bay View Place, P.O. Box 1147
    Pale San Vitores Road, P.O. Box 3520
    Agana, GU 96910
    Phone: (671) 646-5278

Marianas Visitors Bureau
P.O. Box 861
Saipan, CM, Mariana Islands 96950
Phone: (670) 234-8327

Puerto Rico Tourism Company
P.O. Box 025268, Dept. H
Miami, Fl. 33102-5268
Phone: (212) 541-6630
Toll Free:
1-800-223-6530

U.S. Virgin Islands
Division of Tourism
Box 6400, VITIA
Charlotte Amalie, ST. Thomas USVI 00801
Phone: (809) 774-8784
Toll Free:
1-800-372-8784

Appendix B
Canadian Provincial
Tourist Offices

The following list of Canadian provincial Offices of Tourism will send information on travel, sight-seeing, accommodations and special events. If you wish material on particular localities, events or activities, let them know and they will usually send that, too. The prefix 1-800 indicates a toll-free number from mainland USA and Canada with some exceptions for Alaska, the Yukon and the Northwest Territories.

ALBERTA

Travel Alberta
  Vacation Counselling
  15th Floor
  10025 Jasper Avenue
  Edmonton, Alberta
  Canada T5J 3Z3
  Phone: (403) 427-4321
  Toll Free:
    1-800-222-6501 (from Alberta)
    1-800-661-8888 (from mainland USA and Canada)

BRITISH COLUMBIA

Tourism British Columbia
  Parliament Buildings
  Victoria, British Columbia
  Canada V8V 1X4
  Phone: (604) 387-1642
  Toll Free:
    1-800-663-6000 (from mainland USA and Canada)

MANITOBA

Travel Manitoba
  Department 9020, 7th Floor
  Winnipeg, Manitoba
  Canada R3C 3H8
  Phone: (204) 945-3777
  Toll Free:
    1-800-665-0040, ext. 20 (from mainland USA and Canada)

NEW BRUNSWICK

Tourism New Brunswick
    P.O. Box 12345
    Fredericton, New Brunswick
    Canada, E3B 5C3
    Phone: (506) 453-2377
    Toll Free:
        1-800-442-4442 (from New Brunswick)
        1-800-561-0123 (from mainland USA and Canada)

NEWFOUNDLAND AND LABRADOR

Department of Development and Tourism
    P.O. Box 2016
    St. John's, Newfoundland
    Canada A1C 5R8
    Phone: (709) 576-2830
    Toll Free:
        1-800-563-6353 (from mainland USA and Canada)

NORTHWEST TERRITORIES

TravelArctic
    Yellowknife, Northwest Territories
    Canada X1A 2LR
    Phone: (403) 873-7200
    Toll Free:
        1-800-661-0788 (from mainland USA and Canada)

NOVA SCOTIA

Department of Tourism
    P.O. Box 456
    Halifax, Nova Scotia
    Canada B3J 2R5
    Phone: (902) 425-5781

Toll Free:
    1-800-565-7105 (from Nova Scotia,
    Prince EdwardIsland and New Brunswick)

Nova Scotia Tourist Information Office
    136 Commercial Street
    Portland, Maine 04101
    USA
    Toll Free:
        1-800-492-0643 (from Maine)
        1-800-341-6096 (from mainland USA and Canada)

ONTARIO

Ontario Travel
    Queen's Park
    Toronto, Ontario
    Canada M7A 2E5
    Phone: (416) 965-4008
        (416) 965-6027
    Toll Free:
        1-800-ONTARIO (from mainland USA and Canada)

PRINCE EDWARD ISLAND

Department of Tourism and Parks
    Visitor Services Division
    P.O. Box 940
    Charlottetown, Prince Edward Island
    Canada C1A 7M5
    Phone: (902) 368-4444
    Toll Free:
        1-800-565-7421 (from New Brunswick and Nova Scotia -
        March 15 to October 31)
        1-800-565-9060 (east of the Mississippi River)

QUEBEC

Tourisme Quebec
    C.P. 20 000
    Quebec (Quebec)
    Canada G1K 7X2
    Phone: (514) 873-2015
    Toll Free:
        1-800-361-5405 (from Quebec)
        1-800-361-6490 (from Ontario and the Atlantic Provinces)
        1-800-443-7000 (from the eastern USA)

SASKATCHEWAN

Tourism Saskatchewan
    1919 Saskatchewan Drive
    Regina, Saskatchewan
    Canada S4P 3V7
    Phone: (306) 787-2300
    Toll Free:
        1-800-667-7538 (from Saskatchewan)
        1-800-667-7191 (from mainland USA and Canada)

YUKON

Tourism Yukon
    P.O. Box 2703
    Whitehorse, Yukon
    Canada Y1A 2C6
    Phone: (403) 667-5340

Appendix C
Foreign Tourist Offices in the USA

More than 200 national tourist offices are located in the USA. These offices will send you an assortment of helpful travel materials about their particular country. Those listed below are the ones exchangers are likely to find most useful. Where several branches of a national tourist office are located in the USA, an east coast and a west coast branch have been listed for the sake of brevity.

AUSTRALIA

Australian Tourist Commission
    489 Fifth Avenue, 31st Floor
    New York, NY 10017
    Phone: (212) 687-6300

Australian Tourist Commission
    2121 Avenue of the Stars, Suite 1200
    Los Angeles, CA 90067
    Phone: (213) 552-1988

AUSTRIA

Austrian National Tourist Office
    500 Fifth Avenue
    New York, NY 10110
    Phone: (212) 944-6880

Austrian National Tourist Office
    11601 Wilshire, Suite 2480
    Los Angeles, CA 90025
    Phone: (213) 477-3332

BELGIUM

Belgian National Tourist Office
    745 Fifth Avenue
    New York,NY 10151
    Phone: (212) 758-8130

CZECHOSLOVAKIA

Cedok-Czechoslovakia Travel Bureau
    10 East 40th Street
    New York, NY 10016
    Phone: (212) 689-9720

DENMARK

Danish Tourist Board
655 Third Avenue
New York, NY 10017
Phone: (212) 949-2333

Danish Tourist Board
8929 Wilshire Boulevard
Beverly Hills, CA 90211
Phone: (213) 854-1549

FINLAND

Finnish Tourist Board
655 Third Avenue
New York, NY 10017
Phone: (212) 949-2333

Finnish Tourist Board
1900 Avenue of the Stars, Suite 1070
Los Angeles, CA 90067
Phone: (213) 277-5226

FRANCE

French Government Tourist Office
610 Fifth Avenue
New York, NY 10020
Phone: (212) 757-1125

French Government Tourist Office
9454 Wilshire Boulevard
Beverly Hills, CA 90212
Phone: (213) 271-6665

GERMANY

German National Tourist Office
   747 Third Avenue, 33rd Floor
   New York, NY 10017
   Phone: (212) 308-3300

German National Tourist Office
   444 South Flower, Suite 2230
   Los Angeles, CA 90071
   Phone: (213) 688-7332

GREAT BRITAIN

British Tourist Authority
   40 West 57th Street
   New York, NY 10019
   Phone: (212) 581-4708

British Tourist Authority
   350 South Figueroa, Suite 450
   Los Angeles, CA 90071
   Phone: (213) 628-3525

GREECE

Greek National Tourist Office
   645 Fifth Avenue
   New York, NY 10022
   Phone: (212) 421-5777

Greek National Tourist Office
   611 West Sixth Street, Suite 1998
   Los Angeles, CA 90017
   Phone: (213) 626-6696

HUNGARY

Hungarian Tourist Board
  One Parker Plaza, Suite 1104
  Fort Lee, NJ 07024
  Phone: (201) 592-8585

IRELAND

Irish Tourist Board
  757 Third Avenue, 19th Floor
  New York, NY 10017
  Phone: (212) 418-0800

ISRAEL

Israel Ministry of Tourism
  350 Fifth Avenue
  New York, NY 10118
  Phone: (212) 560-0605

Israel Government Tourist Office
  6380 Wilshire Avenue
  Los Angeles, CA 90048
  Phone: (213) 658-7462

ITALY

Italian Government Travel Office
  630 Fifth Avenue
  New York, NY 10111
  Phone: (212) 245-4822

Italian Government Travel Office
  360 Post Street
  San Francisco, CA 94108
  Phone: (415) 392-5266

JAPAN

Japan National Tourist Organization
630 Fifth Avenue, Suite 2101
New York, NY 10111
Phone: (212) 757-5640

Japan National Tourist Organization
One Wilshire Building
624 South Grand, 2640
Los Angeles, CA 90017
Phone: (213) 623-1952

LUXEMBOURG

Luxembourg National Tourist Office
801 Second Avenue
New York, NY 10017
Phone: (212) 370-9850

MEXICO

Mexican Government Tourism Office
405 Park Avenue, Suite 1002
New York, NY 10022
Phone: (212) 755-7261

Mexican Government Tourism Office
10100 Santa Monica Boulevard, Suite 224
Los Angeles, CA 90067
Phone: (213) 202-8150

NETHERLANDS

Netherlands Board of Tourism
355 Lexington Avenue, 21st Floor
New York, NY 10017
Phone: (212) 370-7367

Netherlands Board of Tourism
    90 New Montgomery Street, 3rd Floor
    San Francisco, CA 94105
    Phone: (415) 543-6772

NORWAY

Norwegian Tourist Board
    655 Third Avenue
    New York, NY 10017
    Phone: (212) 949-2333

PORTUGAL

Portuguese National Tourist Office
    590 Fifth Avenue
    New York, NY 10036
    Phone: (212) 354-4403

SPAIN

Tourist Office of Spain
    665 Fifth Avenue
    New York, NY 10022
    Phone: (212) 759-8822

Tourist Office of Spain
    8383 Wilshire Boulevard, Suite 960
    Beverly Hills, CA 90211
    Phone: (212) 658-7188

SWEDEN

Swedish Tourist Board
655 Third Avenue
New York, NY 10017
Phone: (212) 949-2333

SWITZERLAND

Swiss National Tourist Office
608 Fifth Avenue
New York, NY 10020
Phone: (212) 757-5944

Swiss National Tourist Office
260 Stockton Street
San Francisco, CA 94108
Phone: (415) 362-2260

YUGOSLAVIA

Yugoslav National Tourist Office
630 Fifth Street
New York, NY 10111
Phone: (212) 757-2801